John Kent

The Divine Being as Revealed by Himself

John Kent

The Divine Being as Revealed by Himself

ISBN/EAN: 9783337779078

Printed in Europe, USA, Canada, Australia, Japan

Cover: Foto ©Lupo / pixelio.de

More available books at **www.hansebooks.com**

THE

DIVINE BEING

As Revealed by Himself;

OR,

The Reality of Things

AS TAUGHT IN

THE HOLY SCRIPTURES.

By John Kent, Trenton, N. J.

TRENTON, N. J.:
MacCrellish & Quigley, Steam Book and Job Printers.
1877.

Entered according to the act of Congress, in the year 1877,
BY JOHN KENT,
in the Office of the Librarian of Congress, at Washington, D. C.

All Rights reserved.

AUTHOR'S NOTE.

In the production of this, the author has not only rigidly confined himself to the realities of the Sacred Volume, but, in order to simplify the facts presented, has, in a measure, conformed to Scriptural phraseology, and, by dividing the work into fifty distinct parts, has divested it of even the semblance of complexity. So that, though it is one compact, and each article forms a legitimate member of the whole, each article may be considered as a distinct part. Hence, while its open form will not make it any the less acceptable to the penetrating and retentive mind, it will shorten the task of those less gifted, and facilitate the comprehension of all. Yet, while each part may be read as a distinct article, it is certainly best to know the end before the beginning is positively sanctioned or fully condemned.

PREFACE.

It is no uncommon thing for men to conceive the idea of being the author of something agreeable to their particular theories, whether ecclesiastical or scientific, and then to work in accordance with the preconceived notions or prejudices which prompted the undertaking, thus laying their foundation wherever it may happen to suit, and extending their fabric to whatever dimensions may be most convenient. And this course has been more particularly confined to those who, of late days, have endeavored to place themselves before the world as the expounders of the Holy Word; who seem to teach as though they had forgotten that God's Word is still extant, and as though they had never known that it is its own interpreter, and that, notwithstanding all the mystifying, perverting, and all the absurdities that are presented to the world as Scripture, the Word of God is still the same. But the reader of this will soon discover that its contents, instead of being the offspring of some sectarian research, are what the plain language of Scripture teaches; that it is the Word of God as God has spoken it ; that it teaches concerning God as God has revealed Himself unto us; and that it treats of man according to that which man is; that its discrimination between men and angels, between the natural life and the spiritual life, between saint and sinner, between body and soul, and soul and spirit, and all its peculiar features, are not only in harmony with, but are the plain teachings of Scripture; and that the Scriptures, unmixed with the erroneous teachings of man, are perfect harmony. And in order to more clearly display this harmony and expose the erroneous teachings referred to, it has been an object of special attention to avoid that accumulation of evidence and unnecessary references which call the mind from the regular course of the subject and are both embarrassing and tedious. And considering that all are or may be easily informed concerning chapter and verse of the particular passages quoted, and regarding it as necessary that all should search and see whether these things are so, it seems to be more of a display of frankness and wisdom to induce this search than to load a work with unnecessary or useless materials. But because this is the case, it must not be inferred that there has been a leaf unturned, or that there is any Scripture omitted for want of harmony, or that there is anything herein contained which will not harmonize with any or all other Scripture; neither should any suppose that the author is not prepared to answer for all that is herein contained, or to whatever it may call forth. For it is not the result of a few months' labor, nor the surface work of years, but the deep fathoming of the fountain of truth, through many years of solitary study that has been unchained and free from sectarianism, and governed only by the teachings of the Holy Spirit and the dictates of reason and common sense.

TO THE CHRISTIAN.

And when I say Christian, I mean a disciple of the Lord Jesus Christ: one who has been "begotten with the truth," and "born not of blood, nor of the will of the flesh, nor of the will of man, but of God"; one who has realized the enlightening power of the Holy Spirit pointing him to the "Lamb of God that taketh away the sin of the world"; one who realized his lost condition while in a state of sin; one who has realized that for Christ's sake his sins have been forgiven, and that he is reconciled to God; one who has realized that he has "passed from death unto life because he loves the brethren, and because that God hath given unto him of His holy spirit"; one who has "put off the old man with his deeds," and become a new creature in Christ Jesus; one who believes that "the Scripture of old came not by man, neither by the will of man, but that holy men of God spake as they were moved by the Holy Ghost"; one who has embraced the life and teachings of Christ, and the teachings of the apostles, as an all-sufficient and only rule of faith and practice. Hence, as this embraces the reality of the Christian, it is not for him to learn, but to remember, that the Scriptures are the Word of God; and that the Word of God is what teaches us who and what God is, and that whatever the Word tells us He is, that is what He is; for He alone can tell us who He is or what He is. So that, as He is the one and only living and true God, and is just that which He has revealed Himself to be in His own Holy Word, to believe, as so many do, that He is a being so very different from that which He has revealed Himself to be, seems more like believing in some other God than it does like believing in Him; therefore, it is for all to believe that God is just the being that He has revealed Himself to be, and that to believe or teach differently from this, is to believe or teach falsely: as much so, at least, as to believe or teach falsely in any other respect.

And, again, we should remember that we have a right to believe that God is just the being that He tells us He is, and that we have no right to believe anything to the contrary. For if we reject God as He has revealed Himself unto us, and believe in some other sort of Deity, then our faith is in that something else. But if we believe in God as He has revealed Himself unto us, then our faith and hope is in God. And inasmuch as all that we know of our own origin is derived from the Scriptures, and inasmuch as it is God who has revealed unto us the creation, the manner of creation, and the materials of which man was created, to reject this knowledge is as positively rejecting the Word of God as rejecting any other part of it would be.

And if we arrogate to ourselves a nature which does not belong to us, we are certainly denying the truth as revealed in God's Word concerning our nature. And if we clothe ourselves with an attribute that belongs to God, we are not only rejecting the Scriptures, but adorning ourselves with that of which we have robbed Him. Hence, it is for all who love God to adhere with the utmost stability to the plain teachings of the Divine Being as revealed by Himself in His own Holy Word.

TO THE INFIDEL OR SKEPTIC.

The question with you is not as to whether this is true or whether it is false, but the question with you should be, is this which is herein contained in reality the teachings of Scripture? For your free agency places you on the same basis of responsibility, and gives you the privilege of doubting the Scriptures, the same as it gives me and others the privilege of believing them. For "Faith cometh by hearing," that is, comes through or is created by hearing the facts in the case. But it should be remembered that while it is in perfect harmony with reason and common sense to believe, in accordance with the evidence concerning and the truthfulness of that which is presented, to doubt or reject according to the will or wishes is just as inconsistent with that same reason and common sense. So that if we believe contrary to the truth, it is foolishness; and if we disbelieve or reject contrary to the truth, it is just as foolish. And, inasmuch as you doubt the Scriptures, of which this treats, it would be contrary to the teachings of this volume to suppose you under the necessity of believing it, any farther than the harmony and plain truthfulness of its pages might remove from your mind the idea that the erroneous or absurd doctrines that are so prevalent at the present day are the teachings of Scripture, and so far as it affects your reason and is capable of convincing you of the reality of things as taught in the Holy Scriptures.

WHAT THIS LITTLE VOLUME TEACHES.

This volume teaches that in the Sacred Scriptures are revealed the will and workings of Him whose name is Jah, or Jehovah. It teaches that the Scriptures mark out the path of the Christian, and show the infidel his situation. It shows that the Scriptures teach us, in the plainest language, that Jesus Christ was the Son of God, simply because God was His Father; and that Jesus Christ was God, simply because His Father was God; and that all Jesus Christ was or is, His Father, Jehovah, made Him. It shows that the Scriptures teach us, in the most comprehensive manner, that man is the image of his Creator, and that God is a personal being, in likeness or form resembling man; and that the operations of the Holy Spirit are the reachings out, the goings forth of God, who comprehendeth all things within the scope of His own personal self. It shows that the Father and Son are two distinct beings, and that their oneness exists in the reality of the nature of God being one of the natures of Jesus Christ, in which nature there is no separation. It shows that the Scriptures teach us that before man was created it was determined that he should be a free agent;

that man became a sinful being by choice and not necessity, and that the foreordaining of Christ was not positive in its nature, but was a provision made in man's behalf in case that he should fail to use his liberty in accordance with the Divine will. It teaches that the whole plan of salvation, though completed before the creation of man, is in perfect harmony with his free agency, from the day that he was created to the day of judgment. It teaches that Christ, as the Word, was not in the beginning, and shows that the being manifested in the flesh, His being in the world and the world being made by Him; His being sent unto the world; His being rich and becoming poor, were in perfect harmony with the fact that His first existence was when He was born of the Virgin Mary. It shows that though He is equal with God, He is not, never was, and never can be equal to Him. It shows that Christ being glorified that he might glorify His Father, and His being glorified with His Father's own self, are two things and transpired at two particularly different periods. It shows that the family of which Jesus was the first-born Son, was composed of at least nine persons. It shows that the Scriptures teach us that the union of the Divine nature with that of humanity constituted the existence of Jesus Christ, and that though the Virgin Mary was no more the mother of God than she was the mother of her own existence, she was the mother of all that Jesus Christ was. It shows that the Scriptures teach that there is no immortality in man, that faith is an inherency of our nature, and that predestination, as taught by those who are termed predestinarianists, is a scandal against the Almighty. It simplifies the question of the resurrection, and presents its practicability plainly before the eyes of man. It shows that the mind is not the spirit, and that the breath of life and the physical organism is what, and all that, constitutes the soul. It shows the reality of conversion, the folly of doubts, the sense and necessity of communion, the origin, nature and necessity of baptism, and shows the difference between baptism and sprinkling. It shows that the Scriptures teach us that the soul and spirit are two, and that they show us the difference between them. It treats of the judgment and the Judge, of the devil or Satan and hell, and of the finale of the earth, the righteous and the wicked. It shows how it was that Moses was at the transfiguration, and how the spirits are in prison. It analyzes the question of Christ's answer to the thief, and shows the nature of the case in regard to those who had fallen asleep. It shows the consistency of accepting the parable of the rich man and Lazarus as figurative, and shows that the earthly house of our tabernacle is the world in which we live. It shows what the Scriptures teach us concerning Melchisedec, and how Christ is a priest afer his order; that Christ is personally present at the right hand of the Father, and that spiritually He is present with His saints. It shows what the apostles knew about the nature of Christ, and the reality of their faith in Him; and closes with the death and the nature of the death of the Son of God, who was begotten by Himself and born of the Virgin Mary; and plainly shows through all this course that the mystical teachings concerning the Divine Being, the nature of Jesus Christ, the nature of man, and of the future state, are mythological in their origin, heretical in their nature, and are in direct antagonism with the realities of the Holy Scriptures.

Jesus Christ, the Son of God and the Son of Man.

Jesus Christ was the Son of God, because God was His Father; for this reason and no other. Jesus Christ was God because His Father was God; for this reason and no other. And upon these facts Jesus based His claims to Divinity, first, to being the Son of God because God was His Father; secondly, to being God because His Father was God; and, for the same reason, He thought it not robbery to make Himself equal with God. He was not man because God was His Father, but because the Virgin Mary was His mother. And, with respect to the nature of Christ, it is as essential to know that He is man, as it is to know that He is God. And, when we look at the positiveness of His humanity, the fact that He was born of the Virgin Mary, grew up in the family of Joseph, was associated with His brethren and sisters, learned the carpenter's trade, lived to be about thirty years old, then traversed the land of Judea for three years, preaching the Gospel of the Kingdom, laboring in traveling, becoming hungry and thirsty, eating and drinking; seeing all this in Jesus, and knowing that it is the result of His being the offspring of a woman, the case with respect to His humanity is settled. And why should it be any the less clear and positive that

He is God, being the Son of God, than it is that He is man, being the son of man? For the wonderful development as the result of His being the Son of God, manifested His Divinity in the same reality that the foregoing did His humanity. And if His being the son of Mary would make Him man, surely His being the Son of God would make Him God. And thus it is that He is God, and thus it is that He is man. And as regards the humanity of Christ, His death does not annul it in the least sense, for the fact that He was man, is man, and ever will be man, God has shown in the clearest manner, when it is declared that " There is one God, and one mediator between God and man, the *man* Christ Jesus," and when He declares that " He hath appointed a day in the which He will judge the world in righteousness by that *man* whom He hath ordained." As regards his humanity, God created Jesus Christ, thus making Him a part of Mary, a part of man ; as regards His Divinity, He imparted to Him His own nature, thus making Him a part of Himself, a part of God. For we do not say that God creates God, but He creates man, and thus He created Jesus; but in that He is His son, He is the only begotten, and thus a part of Himself. Now, if God, in creating Jesus, imparted to Him His own nature, which it is impossible to be otherwise than that He did, and thereby made Him part of Himself, God, why should it be considered strange that He of omniscient nature should look to the glory of that nature, and desire the sufferings to be over through which He had to pass, and to be crowned with the glory which His Divine nature ultimately required, and which it had with the Father before the world was? Nevertheless, it is not likely that it will not be considered strange, that Jesus is God simply because His Father is God, but the fact must not be lost sight of that He is man, simply because He is the son of Mary. Again, with respect to the nature of Christ, it is well to know that He was not only known as a man and called a man, but that His own claims to humanity were just as definite as His claims to Divinity. For, when He questioned His disciples concerning His nature, He said: "Who say they that I, the Son of Man, am?" Here, as though He feared that they would fail to declare His humanity, or do as many others might have done, say that He was not a man but a god, He cuts it short and makes it necessary for them first to understand that He is a man, and then to tell Him who this man is. And thus His own lips affirmed His humanity, as positively as the wonderful miracles which He performed confirmed the fact that He was Divine. And when the Son of God stood before Pilate it was the Son of Mary that stood there. And when the Son of Mary was nailed to the cross it was the Son of God that was nailed there. And when He was laid in the tomb it was their son that was laid or buried there; and when He arose it was this same being, as literally as when He stood before Pilate. For the evidence that He gave of Himself after His resurrection, was that He was not a spirit, but flesh and bone. And it is evident that without His humanity He could not have been Christ, any more than He could have been Christ without His Divinity, neither before His death nor after His resurrection. For "The mediator between God and man is the man Christ Jesus." But it must be remembered that He is God in the same reality that He is man, and that His claims to Divinity are as clear as His claims to humanity. And in anticipating His death He did not allow this to be lost sight of, for, saith He, "I have power to lay down my life, and I have power to take it again." Man can lay down his life but he cannot take it again. Moreover, the inharmonious view of the resurrection of Jesus Christ does not exist in the facts in the case, for the fact that Jesus had power to take His life again does not interfere with the fact that God raised Him from the dead. For, in either case, whether it were the Father that raised Jesus from the dead, or whether Jesus took His life again, as He said He had power to take it, does not interfere with the facts in the case, but shows the inseparable unity of the Father and Son, as existing in the Divine nature of Jesus, as imparted to Him by the Father, when He was begotten of the Holy Ghost.

Jesus Christ what God, His Father, made Him.

All that Jesus Christ was, His Father, Jehovah, made Him, first by imparting to Him His own nature when He was begotten, and thus making Him God as Himself, and thenceforth bestowing upon Him all that power and dignity that is embraced in the terms "all power," "all the fullness of God." "For it pleased the Father that in Him should all fullness dwell." But it does not follow, that because in Him dwells all the fullness of the Godhead, that he is that Godhead whose fullness dwells in Him. And because all power is given unto Him of His Father, it does not follow that He is that Father who gave Him that power. And what can manifest the essence of absurdity in a more conspicuous form than to say that Jesus Christ is the Son of God, and then to say that He is that God whose son He is? Yet it is evident that the theory that embraces the idea that in Christ dwells all that is God must necessarily embrace all the absurdity of the foregoing. But, for the present leaving these erroneous teachings where they exist, and adhering to the Scriptures, we see that it pleased the Father that in Him should all fullness dwell (but if it had not pleased the Father it would surely have been otherwise); that He should be all that was man, and in reality God. And thus He could be God with God, and man with man, and through His humanity He could be in sympathy with man, and through His Divinity He could be in harmony with God, the Father. Thus we see that He is all that is dignity, might and power, except that His Father is greater than He, and that all this miraculous working has been brought about through the will and working of Him whose name is Jah or Jehovah.

For if God had had five sons, instead of one, each of them would have been God in the reality of God's own nature; and each one would have been the son of God, just as Jesus Christ was His Son, and each one of them would have been the Eternal, just as much as Jesus was the Eternal. That is, if God had had four sons before Christ was born, and each had been born under the same circumstances, (for if God could have one son, He could have five or ten,) and then Christ had been born, just as He in reality was, He would have been the Son of God precisely the same as the other four were, and would have been no more the Eternal God than they were. And thus we see that the reality of God in Christ was simply the Divine nature of His Father, and that, being of that nature, it could not be otherwise than that He was God, just as it could not be otherwise than that He was man, being of the nature of His mother, Mary.

God a Personal Being.

The teachings of many concerning the Divine Nature or the Divine Being is so nearly or exactly the reverse of the knowledge that He has given us of Himself, that it seems more like striving to destroy the truth than it does like an effort to maintain it. For there is about as much consistency in the teachings of many upon this subject as there is in saying that black is white, or that white is white, and that black is white, too. For the question of mystery, as regards the Divine Being, exists in that which it hath not pleased Him to reveal unto us concerning Himself; but that which it hath pleased Him to reveal unto us is not mystery, but revelation, for revelation is mystery revealed. As for example, Paul says that "Without controversy great is the mystery of Godliness;" but in the next few sentences he explains the mystery, and it becomes a revelation. Thus the teachings of man and the teachings of Scripture differ. Man teaches that God is a being without body and parts, but the word of God teaches exactly the contrary, for when Moses desired to see God, God told him that no man could see His face and live. Thus, if God had told Moses that He was a Personal Being, there would have been but a shadow of difference between telling him this and telling him that "he could not see His face and live," and it would not have been any the more positive than the fact that "God passed him on the mount so that Moses saw His hinder parts." So that God did not only tell Moses, but also showed him, that He was a Personal Being. Now, if I were to make it appear that God is a different Being from that which He hath revealed Himself to be in His own Holy Word, I would be a liar against God, for I would be representing Him to be that which He is not. Now, when God said that He created man in His own image, He meant that that man which He created was the image of Himself, not of His spirit, or His holiness, or of any of His attributes, for he is a creature that can represent no such an existence, neither is there any such image attributed to him by Divine authority; but it is His person that man is the image of, and man personal that is His image. And if man were not the image of God—and this is to be determined by the Scriptures, which are the only source from whence we derive the evidence concerning it—it would be necessary for the language of the Scriptures to be in quite a different form, or that it should be such as to convey the idea that he was not the image of his Creator. Now, the plain unincumbered teachings of Scripture concerning it is, that God proposed to make man in His own image, and that that image was to be the image of others besides Himself, because, says He, "Now let us make man in our image." And so it is evident that there were those who bore His image before man was created, and hence it is not so wonderfully strange that man should have been created in the image of the Almighty. For the Scriptures teach us in the plainest language that man is not inferior to the angels, and it might have been some of these to whom man is not inferior, to whom He said, "Now let us make man in our image." For if the angels had been made in the image of God they would have been the image of Him, and so they could have created man in their own image; that is, God and the angels could have created man in their image, and then he would have been the image of them both. Hence, in order to carry out the idea that man is not the image of God, it would be necessary that the Scriptures should read thus, or similar: Now let us make man, not as I made you, in My own image, for I would not have such a being to be the image of Me. So man was made of the dust of the ground, but not in the image of God, for he was too mean a creature to bear any resemblance to Him. This is simply the opposite of the truth as recorded in Genesis, by which that truth must be supplanted before it can be made to appear that man is not the image of Jehovah, his Creator. And hence, when He said, in the likeness of God made He man, He meant that that being which He had made was the likeness of Himself. Therefore, if we know anything about the Word of God, we know that it says that He created man in His own image, and we know that Adam begat a son in his likeness, after his own image. Now, if Adam was not a likeness of God, Seth was not a likeness of Adam. So, if we reject the one we must reject the other, and then we must reject the language that conveys to us the knowledge of God, and the only means by which we are to know anything about the Creator whatever. And if we reject the knowledge which God has given us of Himself and of the creation of man, and the beginning of all things, it seems more like a farce to believe the rest than it does like the *result* of the operations of a sound mind or a pure heart.

And in continuing this all-important subject, another significant fact with respect to the creation of man is brought to view in the commandment of God to Noah, when He says: "Whoso sheddeth man's blood, by man shall his blood be shed, for in the image of God made He him." And here, also, is brought to view the great dignity or the greatness of the being, man, in that he is created in the image of God; and the truth, as it were, reflects back on itself, and shows forth in double clearness the fact that God, Jehovah, the Father of Jesus Christ, is not only a spiritual, but a Personal Being, in likeness or form resembling man. And the shallow conceptions of many in regard to the Divine Being, might well be taught as a mystery, for the great mystery that they present to the world concerning Divinity, seems much better suited to mythology or morbid imagination, than it does to anything upon the face of Scripture, and is so foreign to consistency that it would be well if it were altogether mystery. Thus, in this case, it is the same as in all similar ones, God presenting His truths, and men contradicting or perverting them; thus it ever has been, and thus it is now; for instead of men striving to unfold the truth, they are striving to cast a mist upon it, as though they were afraid of it themselves and afraid lest others should see and believe it for themselves. And it is becoming more and more evident every day, that upon this one all-important subject rests a mighty weight of importance, that now is and will henceforth affect the eternal interests of mankind, by leading them through the harmonious channel of Scripture truth, or driving them into infidelity by mystifying, perverting and hiding the truth, and presenting in its stead their own paltry opinions, the views of certain fanciful church orators, erroneous creeds, willful pervertsons, and even such ideas or notions as are disgusting to common sense. Yet, notwithstanding all this heretical teaching, it does not follow that there is not that more sober-minded, sound-thinking, truth-loving class in the world, whose devotion to Scripture enables them to lay hold of the truth with unbroken faith, and receive and believe it as it is.

And now the further consideration of the subject points to the language of James, who, in speaking of the tongue, says that "Therewith bless we God, even the Father; and therewith curse we men which are made after the similitude of God." And if it hath pleased the Almighty to create man after the similitude of Himself, why should man be such a stubborn or perverse creature as to contradict the similarity that exists between himself and his Creator, when it is God Himself who tells us that thus He hath made him. Moreover, the Apostle, in speaking of God's dear Son, says that "He is the image of the invisible God." Now, we know that the Son of God is the Man Christ Jesus, and we know that the Invisible God is His Father, and we know that it would be impossible for Christ to be the image of His Father unless His Father was a being whom Christ, as His image, could represent. Yet, Paul, in his epistle to the Hebrews, sweeps every shadow from the face of the subject, and leaves it as clear as crystal, when he says that "Christ is the express image of His Father's Person." This one sentence is enough of itself to establish the truth of all that has been said upon the subject, and shows forth in the most comprehensible, unmistakable manner that Jehovah, the Father of Jesus Christ, is not only a Spirit, but a Personal Being, whose likeness or form may be seen in the likeness or form of His Son Jesus Christ. Hence, it is as true as Scripture is true, and as plain as language can make it plain, that man personal is the image of his Maker, and that God is a Personal Being in likeness or form resembling man. And the great reason why the life of man is so precious in the sight of God is because he is the image of Him, which is clearly shown by the words: "Whoso sheddeth man's blood, by man shall his blood be shed, for in the image of God made He him." Thus we see that it is the man, that *personal being, that has the blood that can be shed*, that is the image of God. And if it be asked, are all men the image of God? that question is answered distinctly and unmistakably by the Apostle as just quoted, when, speaking of the Son of God, he said that He was "The brightness of His glory, and the express image of His Person." Which is equivalent to saying that that which was brightness and glory in Christ was the brightness and glory of His Father, and that the Person Jesus or Jesus Personal was the express image of His Father's Person. That is, the Son of God, the Son of Mary, the man Jesus, was not only like or similar to, or made after the similitude of God, but that He was the express image of His Father's Person. Hence it is, that to worship a God whose person Jesus Christ is not the express image of, is to worship a God who is not the Father of Jesus Christ, for Jesus Christ is the express image of His Father's Person. And though Jesus might not have been the express image of His brethren, of His disciples, and of those around Him, yet there was no marked dissimilarity, neither was there any imperfection, and hence it is that in the fullest acceptance of the term man is the image of his Creator, and also in the fullest acceptation of the term, God is a Personal Being, in likeness or form resembling man.

God the Father.

To convey to the mind a full, comprehensible view, or to give a clear understanding of the Divine Being, is not to be considered a small thing. And those who would have a clear understanding of the same, must not only perform the shallow task of reading but must allow their minds to take hold of the depth of the subject, instead of skimming its surface, and, laying aside the veil of sectarian prejudice, look the truth full in the face without being afraid to believe it. To enable the mind to comprehend the nature of the Divine Being, there is nothing that can be presented that more clearly illustrates it than that mighty orb, the Sun; yet, when we consider that this is the workmanship of Him of whom we are speaking, even this illustration must be considered a very feeble one. Still, when we lift our eyes towards heaven, and see how this mighty wonder of creation operates, we can learn a lesson that we can get from no other source. For, when we behold it, we see nothing but brightness, nothing but light, and when we go forth in the morning the darkness has vanished before it, and all nature is brightened with its rays of light; and, again, we see its warming, cheering effects upon all creation, and, realizing its salutary effect upon our own bodies and minds, we rejoice at its first appearance in the morning, and are loath to have the storm-cloud hide it from our view. And all these bright beams which illuminate the earth, all this warmth and congeniality, are the reachings forth, the goings out, of the Sun; and though we experience these goings forth of the Sun every day, there is no diminution, no less of that which was the day before or the last year. They are the same bright beams, the same warmth and congeniality, that have been sent forth since the creation.

And similar is the going forth of God For the searching of all things, the existence everywhere, the all-seeing, the all-knowing, and the all-power manifested everywhere and in all things, must come from somewhere; and it comes from that center, His own Personal Self. As in the creation, the Word says that "the Spirit of God moved upon the face of the waters." This is a going out, a going forth, of God; this is a manifestation, not of power only, but of God's own self, who is the power. And David says: "Whither shall I go from Thy Spirit; or whither shall I flee from Thy presence? If I ascend up into heaven, Thou art there. If I make my bed in hell, behold, Thou art there. If I take the wings of the morning, and dwell in the uttermost parts of the sea; Even there shall Thy hand lead me, and Thy right hand shall hold me." Thus David realized the nature of the Divine Being, and gave utterance to these expressions which show forth the goings out of God and His existence everywhere. For there is no division in God, no dismemberment or separation from Himself. Moreover, with respect to everything being manifest in His sight, David gives the clearest evidence, when he says: "If I say surely the darkness shall cover me, even the night shall be light about me. Yea, the darkness hideth not from Thee; but the night shineth as the day. The darkness and the light are both alike to Thee." And if one half-farthing's worth of all to which God has given life cannot escape His notice, it is useless to entertain any idea contrary to that which teaches that everything is manifest in His sight, and that the all-seeing and searching are the goings out of God: "For the Spirit searcheth all things, even the deep things of God. And who knoweth the things of a man but the spirit of man, which is in him; so, also, the things of God knoweth no man, but the Spirit of God." And wherever the Spirit of God is, there He is present. The spirit of man is not the person of man; neither is the Spirit of God the person of God. The spirit of man is not a separate being from himself, neither is the Spirit of God a separate being from Himself. But the goings out of God, the all-knowing, the all-seeing and searching, and the existence or the manifestations of the Spirit of God everywhere, are no separation in the Being, God, but are the goings forth of Jehovah, who comprehends all things within the scope of His own Personal Self.

The Spirit of God.

With respect to the Spirit of God, we know that God spiritually is everywhere. But, considering the nature of things as they now exist, and as they existed before the birth of Christ, it is not only proper but necessary to particularize. And when we get a clear view of the nature of things or the facts of the case in regard to the conception of Jesus Christ by the Virgin Mary, and His being begotten by the Holy Ghost, we see in this a particular manifestation of the Spirit of God; and see that creative power, that miraculous working that shows that it is the presence or being present of His own self, as embraced in the words, "Thou art My Son, this day have I begotten Thee." And, as said the angel, "The Holy Ghost shall come upon thee, and the power of the Most High shall overshadow thee; therefore also that holy thing which shall be born of thee shall be called the Son of God." Here is a particular manifestation of the Spirit and of the power, and we see, as the result of this manifestation, the existence of Jesus Christ, who is the only begotten of the Father, the only begotten Son of God. Hence we see that the manifestation of the Holy Ghost is the spiritual presence of God, and that His spiritual presence is the reaching out, the going forth, of His own personal self. Thus in this we see a particular manifestation of the Spirit of God.

And when John was "sent before to preach the baptism of repentance to the children of Israel," and knew that he was the forerunner of the Holy One, Jesus made His appearance among them, but John knew Him not, and the only way that he was to know Him was by a particular manifestation of the Spirit of God. And when He had been baptized and come up out of the water, "Lo, the heavens were opened unto Him, and he saw the Spirit of God descending like a dove and lighting upon Him, and there came a voice from heaven, saying, 'This is My beloved Son, in whom I am well pleased.'" Thus we see in this manifestation the visible presence of the Spirit of God upon the earth, and the audible voice of God from heaven. And as "God was manifest in the flesh," so He was "justified in the Spirit," that is, proved to be God by the visible presence of the Spirit of God resting upon Him, and the audible voice of the Father, declaring that He was His Son, and that in Him He was well pleased. And after being "led by the Spirit into the wilderness," and being tempted of the devil, and gaining the victory there, behold angels came and ministered unto Him. Thus He was seen of angels. And from thence He went forth to preach to the Jews, and to *be preached* to the Gentiles; and this being fulfilled, together with His being "believed on in the world and received up into glory," the mystery of godliness was finished, and thus the mystery became a revelation. Again, when after the death, resurrection and ascension of the Lord, "The day of Pentecost was fully come, they were all with one accord in one place. And suddenly there came a sound from Heaven as of a rushing mighty wind, and it filled all the house where they were sitting. And there appeared unto them cloven tongues as of fire, and it sat upon each of them. And they were all filled with the Holy Ghost, and began to speak with other tongues as the Spirit gave them utterance." Here is another particular manifestation of the Spirit of God, in the sound from heaven as of a rushing mighty wind, and in the visible cloven tongues as of fire, and in their being all filled with the Holy Ghost. Now the recipients of this manifestation were the Apostles, and this manifestation was a fulfillment of the promise of Christ, for, saith He, "I will pray the Father and He will give you another Comforter that He may abide with you." Thus the Apostles, the chosen ones of Christ, were endowed with power from on high, and thus prepared for the work that was before them. Moreover, we see that this manifestation was the work of Christ, for, saith the Apostle, "He having received of the Father the promise of the Holy Ghost, hath shed forth this which ye now see and hear." For the all-power conferred on Christ embraced also the manifesting of the Spirit as proceeding from Himself. For, as it pleased the Father "that in Him should all fullness dwell," this manifesting of the Spirit is a part of that fullness, and, therefore, we see that in Him "dwells all the fullness of the Godhead bodily." Moreover, we see that this manifesting of the Spirit is the going forth of Christ, who being God by nature, in that He is Jehovah's Son, and having all power conferred upon Him, is the mighty God. And His presence with His church, or His spiritual existence in every one of His saints, is no separation from Himself, but is the reachings out, the going forth of His own self. For who is it that enjoys the presence of the Spirit of God and realizes that he has "Christ in him, the hope of glory," who does not understand it as the connecting link between himself and his Redeemer? Yea, and God dwelling in him, he realizes an existence that reaches from Christ Personal to himself.

According to the foregoing facts, that is, according to the plain teachings of the Word of God, it is not only probable but positive, that in the beginning of creation there was but one God, and that that one is He who has revealed Himself to us in His Word as the living and true God. That Personal Being who, though He had told Moses that he could not see His face and live, nevertheless, passed him on the mount in such a manner as to show Moses His hinder parts; that Personal Being whose Spirit is the Holy Ghost. Hence it is as foolish to contradict the fact that God is a Personal Being as it is to contradict the fact that He is a Spiritual Being. For as the Holy Ghost is the Spirit of God, the Personal Being whom Moses saw when he was on the mount is the God whose Spirit the Holy Ghost is. And hence how plain it is that God is a Personal as well as a Spiritual Being, and that the manifestations of the Spirit of God are the reachings out the goings forth of His own personal self, who is the Lord, Jehovah. And it must be remembered that what has been said concerning the Divine Being, the creation and its results, before the birth of Jesus, is concerning them as prior to the existence of Christ. And that Christ did not exist before He was born of the Virgin Mary, except that when He was born He was God, as imparted to Him by the Father when He begat Him, and thus was God by nature, in which nature there is no separation. And this God or God-nature which He was after He was begotten, is the God or God-nature that He was before the world was. But He was not Christ before the world was, for Christ was the Son of God. And He was not the Son of God before the world was, for His mother was not in existence. And He could not have been the Son of God until God had begotten Him, and this did not take place until the days of Herod, and after the delivery of the message, by the angel, concerning it. And He was not the Son of God until He was the son of Mary, as, said the angel, "therefore that holy thing that shall be born of thee shall be called the Son of God."

The Oneness of the Two Distinct Beings.

Inasmuch as the foregoing teaches that there are two distinct beings in which dwells the one God, it will be well to give particular attention to the Scriptural facts with respect to the particular oneness of the two distinct beings, which facts will be embraced in the consideration of the more difficult passages relating to the subject under their respective heads. But before proceeding any further, it must be remembered that according to that which it hath pleased the Almighty to reveal unto us concerning Himself, it is clear and positive that there is but one Person in the Godhead, or that the Godhead is one Person who is that Personal and Spiritual Being, Jehovah, and that the *Person Jesus* is not in the Godhead, but that the *fullness* of the Godhead is *in Him*, and that though He is God by nature as imparted to Him by the Father, and that in Him dwells all the fullness of the Godhead bodily, that before the birth of Jesus Christ there was but one Being that was God, or that possessed any of the attributes of God, and that Jesus, the Son of God, did not exist any more than Levi did when Abraham met Melchisedec, and "Levi, as it were, paid tithes in Abraham." And now, as the foundation is the first part of all things, and has been the first considered in the foregoing, so now, in its continuance, we can see the foundation of the so-called mystery by tracing it through the facts as presented in the Scriptures, through which we can see that instead of its being what it once was, a partial mystery, it is now a glorious revelation. And the first thing to understand is the great principle or fact upon which our responsibility to God is based, which is so inseparably woven with the truth as revealed in I Peter, i : 20, as presented under the head of free agency and foreordination.

Free Agency and Foreordination.

The idea that foreordination, as presented in the Scriptures, teaches that man is predestined to be saved or to be damned, is not only a falsity, but the reality of the case is exactly the reverse, as is clearly shown in connection with Him "who verily was foreordained before the foundation of the world, but was manifest in these last times." And it is evident that the being foreordained before the foundation of the world, as embraced in the foregoing, is not only consistent with the nature of things as embraced in the plan of salvation, but that it brings within its scope that great and inseparable truth—the fact that man is a free agent. And as this foreordination teaches us concerning things as existing before the foundation of the world, it not only points to the Lamb without blemish and without spot, "who verily was foreordained before the foundation of the world," but necessarily embraces all those facts connected with that foreordination, and places plainly before us the fact that the being foreordained before the foundation of the world was not, as is almost or quite universally supposed, that it was determined before the foundation of the world that Christ should be slain or die for the sins of the world; and that the fall of man and his becoming a sinful being was an inevitable result of his creation. No; but when man was created he was created a free agent, and it would have been impossible for him to have been a free agent and at the same time to have been controlled by a person or power that prevented him from choosing to do evil or to do good.

Hence, when the creation of man was contemplated by the Almighty, and it was determined that he should be what he is, a free agent, the fact that he might choose evil rather than good, was not overlooked by the Almighty. And, as all things were prepared for him in case of his obedience, so was provision made for him in case that he should fall. And this provision was embraced in Him who "was manifest in these last times," and who was "verily foreordained before the foundation of the world," not that man should fall and that He should be slain, but that if man should fall, that then He was to be the ransom, and would die for man. Hence, we see why "God so loved the world that He gave His only begotten Son to die for us." For He did not only love His Son before He was in existence, but He also loved man before he was created, for if He had not, it is certain that He would not have made such wonderful provision for him as was embraced in the sacrifice of His only begotten Son. So it is evident that the free agency of man is older than man himself, for it was determined by the counsel and foreknowledge of his Creator before the foundation of the world. And this free agency stands forth as the manifest dignity or greatness of man, and is the basis of that accountability for which he is to be called to an account at the judgment, by Him who created him and endowed him with this dignifying attribute, and has shown such wonderful love towards him as is manifest in the " gift of His only begotten Son," " who verily was foreordained before the foundation of the world," not that He should die, but that if man should sin that then He was to become the ransom, and die for man.

Jesus Christ's First Existence.*

Lest anything in the foregoing shall be construed to imply that Jesus was God only what is termed spiritually, it will be well to carefully consider and keep in view that which has been said concerning His birth, and that the humanity of Christ had no father but God; that God was the Father of all that Jesus was, and that this is why Jesus is the Son of God. Now, as regards the existence of Christ, we have first the message of the angel to the effect that Christ should be born; secondly, that God would be His Father, and, thirdly, that Mary would be His mother. And these three facts are significant of nothing more or less than the creation of or bringing into existence of the Son of God, Jesus Christ; and it is a fact that does not require any great mind to comprehend, that as Mary was His mother, He would be of the same nature as Mary, and that, as God was His Father, He would be of the same nature as God, His Father. And His being in form a perfect man was in perfect harmony with the case, not only as regards His being the offspring of Mary,

---

*NOTE.—The reader should be careful to remember that it is the realities of the Scriptures to which his attention should be directed, and not sectarian notions.

but as a result of His being the Son of God, for man is the image of his Creator. Hence we see that He was man because Mary was his mother, and God because God was His Father, therefore, it is evident that as Christ was man because Mary was His mother, and God because God was His Father, that His first existence was when He was born of the Virgin Mary, for this was the Son of God, and He never had any other. And He was not God only what is termed spiritually, but the one part of His existence, one part of that of which He was created and constituted His being, was God; and it is evident that as Jesus was God, the God or God-nature that He was, was God always; for as there is but one God this that He is must be a part of that God or God-nature that is one God; and this is in perfect harmony with the words of Jesus, when He says, "the Father that is in Me, He doeth the works," that is, the Father, God, which Jesus was by nature, for there is no God but the Father of Jesus, and the Father was the God, or the God-nature of the Father was the Father that was in Him and did the works. Thus it is plain that Jesus was God as imparted to Him by the Father when He begat Him, and that God in Christ and God the father are identical, and are the same one nature now as before the world was; thus it was that in the man Christ Jesus, God the Father, who was the God-nature of Jesus, was the Father that was in Him and did the works. And thus it is that He is in the Father and the Father in Him. And now, in the consideration of the more difficult passages relating to the subject, it will be seen that instead of these passages casting a mist or doubt upon that which has been said, that they are in perfect harmony with these truths, and are only a continuation of the same; and that the Scriptures are not chaos and mystery, but harmony and revelation.

In the Beginning was the Word.

"In the beginning was the word, and the word was with God, and the word was God. The same was in the beginning with God. All things were made by Him; and without Him was not anything made that was made."—*John, I ch.*, 1*st v.* (In the beginning God was not without that Divinity or Divine nature that was afterward imparted to Jesus, and that God or God-nature that Jesus was, God in the beginning was not without; but that nature was with Him and was a part of Himself).

Now, according to the first verse, the Word, or the Divine nature of Jesus, which was called the Word, was in the beginning, and was with God, and was God, a part of His own nature or self. But after the bringing into existence of the only begotten of the Father, then there was another being who was of the same nature as Himself, whose existence was the result of the union of that nature with that of humanity; and this Divine nature or Divinity is that which was in the beginning with God, and was God, and now is God in Christ. And so nothing that was made was made without Him or this Divine nature that He is, for when they were made this nature was with God and was not in Christ, for then Christ was not in existence.

The World Knew Him Not.

"He was in the world and the world was made by Him, and the world knew Him not."—*John, I ch. 10th v.* It would be very unwise for one to say that the world did not know the man Jesus, a man who had lived to be about thirty-three years old, had spent three years publicly demonstrating the power of God as existing in Himself, and had suffered death upon the cross, through the perfidious workings of a degenerate people, who after His death charged His disciples with having filled Jerusalem with His doctrine. And it is evident that there were few men better known than the man Jesus. Moreover this fact that they knew Him they sat up as a reason for doubting concerning His being the Son of God. As ' Thou, being a man, makest Thyself God." Yet "He was in the world and the world knew Him not." This is the positive assertion of the Apostle, and is certainly correct; and as it is evident that the world knew the man Jesus, who is it that the world did not know? The Word says that "there was a man sent from God, whose name was John. The same came for a witness to bear witness of the light, that all men through Him might believe. Therefore that light which he was not, but which he bore witness to, is He who was in the world and the world knew not, He who was the true light that lighteneth every man that cometh into the world. Here the one mentioned as not known is plainly shown to be the "light that lighteneth every man that cometh into the world." And this light, in which there is no darkness, which is God and is the true light, is the light which was in Jesus, or which Jesus was by nature, and which the world knew not.

The Word was made Flesh.

"The Word was made flesh, and dwelt among us, and we beheld His glory, the glory as of the only begotten of the Father, full of grace and truth."— *John I ch.*, 14*th v.* The Word that was made flesh is the same Word that was in the beginning with God and was God. Therefore, as the Word was God, and there was but one that was God, the Word must have been a part of that same one God, for God is one, whether the Father in the Son or the Son in the Father, it is the same one God. As regards the Father, it is God, Jehovah; as regards the Son, it is God as imparted to Him by the Father. For it was the being that was born of the Virgin Mary that was His Son, and the humanity of Jesus, which He received from His mother, was as much the Son of God as the God-nature of Himself; and thus it is that the Word was made flesh or to exist in the flesh. For when they *beheld His glory they beheld it as the glory of the only begotten of the Father*. Hence we see that the Word became flesh, or in the flesh, by His being begotten of the Father. Therefore, if we speak of the humanity of Christ it is Himself that we speak of; if we speak of His Divinity it is He the same; and if we speak of Him, it is both His humanity and Divinity that we speak of. For as in Him is combined both humanity and Divinity, the one cannot be Him without the other, for the union of these two natures is just what constituted His existence.

I Came Forth from the Father.

"I came forth from the Father and am come into the world: again, I leave the world, and go to the Father."—*John, XVI ch.*, 28*th v.* According to the views of many with regard to this coming forth from the Father, it is construed to imply that Jesus existed before He was born of the Virgin Mary, and that His existence consisted in the Eternal Sonship, or that in some mysterious manner He was God. That is, first He was God, then He was the Eternal Son of God; that is, He was always the Son of God, and this Son was always God, and there never was any God but the Father, and the Father was the living and true God, and the Son was equal to Him. Then this Son, who was always God, notwithstanding that there was no God but the Father, became a man; that is, Jehovah, who alone is God, became the Father of Him whose name was to be called Jesus. Then this Son was the other Eternal Son, and as those who saw Him saw the Father, He was the Father, the Son, and the Eternal Son; and so His being manifest in the flesh embraced all that was God. No wonder that they called it mystery—mystery is no name for it. No wonder that the infidel smiles, and the heathen prefers his own God; no wonder that men are taught to lay aside reason and close their Bibles, that they may embrace such ridiculous absurdity as this. But wonderful, indeed, is it that there are so many who, with open Bibles and free pulpits, embrace and teach this Herculean heresy in its most glaring form. But, away with it, in the Word of God there is no room for any such ideas, but each and every truth is as a bright and shining light, and will emit no such gloom or darkness. So, when Jesus said that He came forth from the Father and came into the world, He meant that He Himself came forth from the Father, and came into the world. And who was this person that spake thus, but the man Christ Jesus, who was begotten of the Father. And hence the saying, I came forth from the Father, just as the Scriptures says: "And when He brought the first begotten into the world, He saith, and let all the angels of God worship Him." Him who came forth from the Father (that is, when He was begotten,) and came into the world. For it was the man Jesus, the Son of God, the Son of Mary, He who came into existence when He was born of the Virgin Mary, that came forth from the Father and came into the world. Then says He, "Again, I leave the world and go to the Father." Here we see that the person who came forth from the Father, and came into the world, is the person who leaves the world and goes to the Father. It was not a shadowing something that existed in mystery, but the Son of God, the Son of Mary, that person who was there and thus addressed His disciples. And there would be just as much consistency in saying that the Capitol at Washington was in existence before the Roman Republic, because the iron of which its dome is constructed was in existence at or before that time, as there would be in saying that Christ was in existence before the foundation of the world, because the God-nature that constituted the Divinity of the being, Jesus Christ, was in existence at and before that time.

For Thou Lovedst Me Before the Foundation of the World.—*John XVII: 24.*

God did not love Jesus simply because He was the Son of Mary, but, more particularly, because He was His own Son. And inasmuch as God so loved the world, or man, as to provide for his salvation through the sacrifice of His only begotten Son, if He have such love towards man before He was created, it is evident that He loved Jesus before He was born or begotten, or, as Jesus said, " before the foundation of the world." For, as He was " foreordained before the foundation of the world," so He was loved before the foundation of the world. For the love that God manifested towards us in the gift of His only begotten Son, being embraced in the being " foreordained before the foundation of the world," this love which He has manifested towards us He had for us before the foundation of the world, or at the time of the foreordaining. And this great love that He had towards us even before our creation, is presented to our view through the fact that He gave His only begotten Son, whom He loved so dearly at that time, to die for us. Hence, the love that He had toward the world, or man, must have preceded the foreordaining, as in Him who was foreordained was manifested this love. Hence, this love existed, and this foreordination was a provision made in consequence of this love. Therefore, as God so loved man before he was created, it is clearly evinced that He loved His only Son before He was born or begotten, or, as Jesus said, " before the foundation of the world."

Sent into the World.

The idea that Jesus was sent from the Divine glory, or that it embraced a separate pre-existence, is quite as absurd as the idea generally entertained concerning His coming forth from the Father. For the one sent was Jesus Christ, and there was no Jesus Christ but the Son of God; and God never had a son except the one that was begotten by Himself and born of the Virgin Mary, and this was the one that was sent. But it has been such an all-absorbing task with the advocates of Christianity to maintain the fact that Christ was Divine, that they seem to have lost sight of the fact that it is just as important to know that He is man as it is to know that He is God. For if Jesus had not been man He could not have wrought our salvation; for the atonement was made by His death. For " God so loved the world that He gave His only begotten Son to die for us." Thus we see that the one who died for us was the one who was begotten of the Father, and born of the Virgin Mary, the one whom the Father sanctified and sent into the world; this one was the person Jesus who was the Virgin's son, and this person was the one who was sent. But He was not sent when He was born, for He was then the helpless infant that needed the strong arms of Joseph to bear Him beyond the reach of the murderous Herod, who sought the young child's life. It is true that He was born, but He was not sent on the mission for which He came into the world, and which constituted His being sent. For He was first to be manifested as man, for it was not that the flesh was to be manifested in God, but that God was to be manifested in the flesh. And that He was first to be manifested as a man is evident from the fact that He was twelve years old before there was any particular manifestation as regards His Divine nature; and after that He was subject to His mother and Joseph, and learned the carpenter's trade; was associated with men, lived, moved and mingled with them and lived as they lived, and was regarded by them as a son, as a brother, as a fellow-mechanic; and, as we understand, was "in favor with God and man." And thus manifested as a man, who had lived to be about thirty years old, He was sent forth upon the mission for which He came into the world. And the fact that that was the time when He was sent, is evident from the fact that John preceded His coming, and said, "There cometh one after me whose shoes I am not worthy to stoop down and unloose." So if He had been sent before that, then He would not have come after John, for John said, "that He might be manifest therefore have I come preaching." And again, John himself was in desert places until his showing unto Israel, and that was while Jesus was being manifested as a man, prior to His being sent forth upon the great mission for which He came into the world. And as Jesus was sent into the world, so John was as truly sent before Him; and the Apostles were sent into the world as really as Jesus was sent. For, saith He, "as Thou hast sent Me into the world, so also have I sent them into the world." And as God sanctified His Son, Jesus, and sent Him into the world, so were the Apostles sanctified through the truth that Jesus taught them, and were sent into the world; and inasmuch as these were sent into the world as He was sent, so it was that He was sent as they were sent. So first "there was a man sent from God, whose name was John," and then the Son of God was sent, and then as He was sent so He sent His twelve Apostles. And hence we see how plainly the truth is presented to us in Gal. IV: 4, "*But when the fullness of the time was come, God sent His Son, made of a woman, made under the law.*" Here we see that as Adam was made at the creation, so Christ was made after that creation, for "when the fullness of the time was come," that is, when the full or proper time came, then God sent forth His Son, not that was made when eternity began, but He who was made thousands of years after the creation began. Not a Son that was always, or always was a Son, but His Son that was made of a woman. For He was made of a woman, and made under the law. And this woman was made hundreds of years after the law was made, and the law was made hundreds of years after the world was made. Hence we see that the Son of God was made, that the time when

He was made was during the existence of the law of Moses, and we also see it positively affirmed that He was "made of a woman," and that this Son that was "made of a woman, made under the law," was the one who was sent.

The One that was Rich, yet Became Poor.

He who, though He was rich, yet for our sakes became poor, that we, through His poverty, might be rich; He who made Himself of no reputation; He who took upon Himself the form of a servant; He who was obedient unto death, even the death of the cross.

When Jesus stood before Pilate, and Pilate questioned Him concerning His being a king, Jesus answered, "Thou sayest that I am a king." And when the shepherds came "seeking for Jesus," they said, "Where is He that is born king of the Jews?" Hence, we see that when Jesus was born, he was born a king. He was the legitimate heir to the throne of David, and at His birth was the rightful sovereign of the kingdom of Israel, and all the glory and resources of that kingdom were His the day that He was born. Moreover, He was not only Humanity, but Divinity; and though it is possible to impoverish Humanity, it is impossible to impoverish Divinity. Again, He was the child that was born unto us, the Son that was given unto us, whose name is Wonderful Counsellor, the Mighty God, the Everlasting Father, the Prince of Peace; He was the one who received the homage of the Shepherds, the one who was "presented with gold, frankincense and myrrh." Therefore, it could not have been otherwise than that Jesus was rich when He was born. And it must be remembered that the poverty of His mother and Joseph, and His being poor, are two things. But it was necessary for us that He should become poor, or as it were poor, just as His "taking upon Himself the form of a servant" was not a servant, but "the form of a servant." For if, through His poverty, we were to be made rich, it is evident that if He had remained rich, we should have remained poor. "Yet for our sakes He became poor," or as it were poor; and this was an act of His own, just as His making Himself of no reputation, and taking upon Himself the form of a servant, was His own act. Hence, we see that as Jesus made Himself of no reputation, but placed Himself on a level with those who were poor, and took upon Himself the form of a servant, it must have been the Son of Mary that acted thus. And the time when this seems to have commenced was when He went down from the feast and was subject to His mother and Joseph, after having been found in the temple disputing with the doctors of the law. For after that He was subject to His parent; and though He might have learned the carpenter's trade with Joseph, it was none the less the form of a servant. Moreover, He was obedient unto death; but this part of the obedience was obedience to His Father, and not to His mother or man. As "Lo I come, in the volume of the book it is written of Me, to do Thy will, oh God." And again, "Not My will, but

Thine be done." Again, in regard to making Himself of no reputation, this was while He was being manifested as a man; for it would require a very elastic faith to believe that Jesus made Himself of no reputation while He was being manifested as God. Moreover, the one who died on the cross was the one that was rich and became poor; that made Himself of no reputation; that took upon Himself the form of a servant; and this was the one that was begotten of the Father, and came into existence when He was born of the Virgin Mary.

The Falsity of Being Equal to God.

The idea that Christ was equal to the Father, is another of those gross perversions called mysteries, that are so foreign to the realities of the Scriptures. For being equal to God, and being equal with Him, are phrases which widely differ in signification. For as Jesus was the Son of God, and His creation or existence was brought about by His Father, it is evident that it would be impossible, according to the nature of the case, for Him to be equal to God the Father. And though the fact that He is equal with God, is in perfect harmony with the nature of things, the idea that He is equal to Him is altogether erroneous, as it is impossible for any person or power to be equal to that person or power that created and sustains it. And this being equal to God is a fabrication of man, destitute of Scriptural support, and is directly contrary to the teachings of Christ, for His claims were to equality with God the Father, but not to being equal to Him; and notwithstanding that He taught and proved to His disciples that he was Divine, and that He and His Father were one, He also taught them that all that He was, and all that He was to be, was, and was to be by the power, and according to the pleasure of His Father, who was greater than He.

The Reality of that which is Taught in Col., I ch., 15th to 18th v.

". Who is the image of the Invisible God, the first-born of every creature?" Here, in speaking of Christ, Paul tells us, positively, that He is not the Eternal God, for if He were the Eternal, He would not be the image of the Invisible God, who is the Eternal, but would be that Eternal God, and this passage would be as flatly nonsense as it would be to say that Paul was the image of himself. And then he adds that "He was the first-born of every creature," and shows us that this being born was being born from the dead; that He who was the beginning was the first-born from the dead; so that this beginning that He was, was begun when He arose from the dead. For surely He never was dead before; so it was then that this beginning began; for there have been many beginnings, of which this is one (17th verse): "And He is before all things, and by Him all things consist." That is, He is before all that followed this beginning or His resurrection. "And by Him all things consist." That is, after He received the gift of the Holy Ghost, and all power was conferred upon Him, and He became the mighty God. For this all things is limited to those things which existed, or were created after His resurrection, or that beginning which commenced at His resurrection. "Whether they be things in heaven or in earth, visible or invisible; whether thrones, dominions, principalities or powers, they were created by Him and for Him." That is, to serve His purpose. "And He is the head of the body, the church, who is the beginning, the first-born from the dead." So that when He was born from the dead, that was His beginning, as this great one, that He might have the pre-eminence, and being the first raised from the dead He was the first, and commenced this dispensation, the consummation of which is to be the resurrection, by Him, of all who are of that number of which He is the first. And as Christ was God, the God that He was, was God in reality. But here it must be remembered, that in the nature of God there is no separation, and that the God-nature of Jesus was the Father in Him. And hence the fact, that as the Father was the God-nature of Jesus, that Father was the one who made the world, for just as the Father that was in Him did the works, just so the Father that was in Him made the worlds. And just as they say that the works spoken of were done by Jesus, just so they say that the worlds were made by Him. But Jesus said that these works were done by the Father, which was in Him, and if He had spoken concerning the worlds it is evident that He would have taught the same concerning them. But Paul understood one by the teaching of the other, and said, "To us there is but one God, even the Father."

Hence the reason why the Apostles ascribe the creating power to Jesus was not the result of any ignorance on their part, but because they understood the nature of God, and knew that as Christ was, in reality, the begotten of the Father, it could not be otherwise than that He was God. And hence the reason why they said, by Him were all things created, was because they believed what Jesus taught them; that is, that the God that He was, was the Father in Him. And hence we see, that instead of the Apostles teaching that Jesus existed before He was born of the Virgin Mary, they show us plainly that it was His Father, Jehovah, that existed, and that by Him were all things created; and the teachings of Jesus not only show us that this is the case, but show us plainly that the works that He did were the works of that same Divine-nature which was imparted to Him when He was begotten, and that as the Father, which was in Him, did the works that He performed here on earth, that that same Father was the creator of all things, and that He also created Him when He was begotten of the Holy Ghost and born of the Virgin Mary.

Christ Glorified with His Father's Own Self.

" And now, O Father, glorify Thou Me with Thine own self, with the glory which I had with Thee before the world was."—*John XVII ch., 5th v.*

In this connection, as in many others, that peculiar trouble occurs which other books are not subject to, that is, the mixing up, by the reader, of times, characters, subjects and so on. For men will read other books and believe that their authors mean what they say, instead of what others may wish it to be, or what they may happen to think, and they will at least read a chapter before they pass sentence upon it. But there are many who will read a sentence in one place in the Scriptures, and then if they find another sentence somewhere else that sounds differently, they condemn the whole, without knowing the connections of either. And the case is no better, or very little, with many who attempt to expound the Scriptures, for their sectarian credulity is about as easily satisfied as the skepticism of the infidel, so that one is about as consistent as the other. But when these times, characters, subjects and so on, are seen in their proper places, and understood with their legitimate connections, that mystic shade that has been cast upon them vanishes away, and these truths are not only to be seen, but shine forth with that brilliancy and force which show that they are not only truths but that they are Divine. So in this text it must be remembered that Christ's glorifying His father and His being glorified with His Father are two things. For, in the first place, Jesus told His Father that He had glorified Him on the earth, and that He had finished the work that He had given Him to do. Thus showing that the glorifying of His Father was wrought by His obedience to His Father, in performing that which the Father had enjoined upon Him. Up to this time Jesus had been devoted to the work of glorifying His Father, and after, as He supposed, He had accomplished that work in its fullest sense, then He desired to be glorified with His Father's own self. Not that he was not by nature God, as the Father was, or that His Divine nature was not of the Father, but because His Father was greater than He. And all these expressions concerning His being glorified are petitions or prayers to the Father. And though God had glorified His name and would glorify it again, the desire of Jesus that He might be glorified with His Father's own self was not granted until after His death and resurrection. For the hour having come when God was to glorify Jesus that Jesus might glorify Him, and the time when the Father was to glorify Jesus with His own self, are two distinct periods. And notwithstanding the fact that Jesus was God by nature, it is evident that He longed for the time of His glorification to arrive, without knowing the exact time when it was to take place. For He who was to bring it to pass was greater than He; and as it was God who imparted the Divine nature to Jesus, He controlled that nature and power, and developed it according to His pleasure. And it was not until after the all-power was conferred upon Jesus, which power embraced the manifesting of the Spirit, that Christ was glorified with His Father's own self; and it was then that He became the mighty God; and thus forever relieved from the humiliation of His natural life, and crowned as the mighty God, He was glorified with His Father's own self, with the glory that His Divine nature had with the Father before the world was.

The Family of Jesus, or How He was Related to Mankind, as Embraced in His Family Connections.

And inasmuch as the truth concerning these connections has been so grossly perverted by those who desire to clothe humanity with the attributes of the Almighty, that they may worship the creature instead of the Creator, who have added to the damnable heresies which constitute their organization, the dogma of the immaculate conception of the Virgin Mary; and to this a still more audacious falsity, by teaching that the mother of Jesus Christ never had a child except Him, and that she was not only a virgin before Christ was conceived, but that she is now, and never was anything else. In view of this audacious scandal against truth and sense, and that the nature of Christ, as embraced in His humanity, may be more easily seen, it is proper to understand the Scriptural facts in regard to these things; and so, in the very first fact that presents itself, we see the utter falsity of the assertion that the Virgin Mary was or is a virgin in any other sense than that in which all other women are or are not virgins. For when Joseph had suspected Mary of infidelity, the "Lord said unto him, fear not to take Mary to thy wife, for that which is conceived in her is of the Holy Ghost. Then Joseph did as the angel of the Lord commanded him, and took unto him his wife, and knew her not until she had brought forth her first-born son." Here is presented the relationship of Joseph to Mary as existing prior to the birth of Christ, and afterwards, as plainly as language can teach it, and shows that Jesus was not the only son of Mary, but that He was her first-born son, which she had before Joseph knew her; and that afterwards he knew his wife, and she had other sons, which were not her first-born, but her second, third, and so on. But this testimony, though positive and sufficient in itself to condemn the idea of Mary's being a virgin after Christ was born, and of Christ being the only son of Mary, it is small compared with that which follows. For Matthew (XIII : 54 to 57) tells us that "when He was come unto His own country, He taught them in their synagogues, insomuch that they were astonished, and said, whence hath this man this wisdom, and these mighty works? Is not this the carpenter's son? is not His mother called Mary, and His brethren, James, Joses, and Simon, and Judas? And His sisters, are they not with us? Whence then hath this man all these things? And they were offended in Him." Here we have recorded, in the plainest language possible, the fact that Mary had five sons and at least two daughters. And the very reason why they rejected Him was because they knew His mother, and that James and Joses and Simon and Judas were His brothers, and that they knew His sisters. And the manner in which they expressed themselves was equivalent to saying, We know His mother, and brothers and sisters, and here He is making Himself the Son of God; He is not the Son of God; He is nothing but a man, for we know His mother, His brothers and sisters. Thus, the very fact that they knew His mother, and that she had these children, and that He was one of them, they sat up as a reason for rejecting Him as the Son of God. Yet, in opposition to all this, the disgusting frivolity is advanced that the sons of Mary were called brethren. But even this is silenced by Mark, who records the circumstance in such a manner as to fit the phraseology exactly to the fact, as recorded in chapter VI, 2d and 3d verses: "And when the Sabbath day was come, He began to teach in the synagogue: and many hearing Him were astonished, saying, from whence hath this man these things, and what wisdom is this which is given unto Him, that even such mighty works are wrought by His hands. Is not this the carpenter, the son of Mary, the *brother* of James, and Joses, and Judas, and Simon, and are not His sisters with us? And they were offended at Him." And the interrogative form in which they expressed the fact that they knew His mother and brothers and sisters, being the most positive and strongest manner in which it could be expressed, shows that they not only knew it, but that the fact that He was the son of Mary and brother of her children, proved satisfactorily to them that He was not the Son of God. Hence, as this was the only reason, or the best that they could give for rejecting Him, and as they gave it there, in public and in His presence, without being contradicted, it leaves the subject without a shadow of doubt. And it is not improbable that, as Jesus was in His own country, and among His own kin, some of those who denied His claims to Divinity had eaten at the same table with Him and His brothers and sisters, or wrought with Him and His brothers in the erection of the same building. Yet, notwithstanding all this, it is asserted that Jesus had no brother except those who were His brethren in the Gospel; and though this idea is so belittling in the eyes of common sense, and displays such willful perversion in the teacher, and such bigoted credulity in the believer, it is advanced as an all-sufficient argument against all the preceding truths, and, though too insignificant in itself to be worthy of consideration, yet, as it constitutes the best they can produce, the nature of the case requires that it should be noticed. And as it is true that Christ had brethren in the Gospel, this same fact makes it positive that He had brethren who were not brethren in the Gospel, but were His own mother's sons. "And these brothers said unto Him, depart hence, and go into Judea, that Thy disciples also may see the works that Thou doest. For there is no man that doeth anything in secret, and he himself seeketh to be known openly. If Thou do these things, show Thyself to the world. *For neither did His brethren believe in Him.*" And these brethren who did not believe in Him were His mother's children, His brothers James, Joses, Simon and Judas; for it was impossible for Him to have had any other brethren who did not believe on Him. For all others who were His brethren, were His brethren in the Gospel, and before they could have been His brethren, they must of necessity have believed on Him; so that, to be His brethren in the Gospel, without believing on Him, was outside of possibility; therefore, it would have been impossible for those who did not believe on Him to have been any other brethren than His natural brethren, the children of Mary, who were James, Joses, Simon and Judas. Hence, it is plain that Mary was a pure virgin at the time that the angel delivered the message, and it is just as plainly taught, and as positively affirmed, that afterwards she became the mother of at least seven children; and thus we see that the relationship of Christ to mankind is not only in part, but in the fullest reality. And in this man should ever glory; for if God so loved the world as to manifest Himself in the flesh by uniting His own nature with that of humanity, how greatly ought it to affect us to praise and thanksgiving; and hence, how basely heretical to make it appear that such an event never took place in reality, and that Christ was the offspring of one who did not possess the infirmities of humanity or the real nature of man; but that He was the offspring of a sort of goddess, who, if not Divine, was so much superior to the daughters of Adam as to be destitute of everything that could bring one of her offspring in sympathy with imperfect, fallen man, and deprive him of that Great High Priest who could be touched with a feeling of his infirmities. And every attempt to destroy the reality of the birth and nature of Christ as a man, conflicts with the reality of His nature as God, (for, if He was not the son of man, He was not the Messiah, and, therefore, was not the Son of God,) for He was one in the same sense that He was the other, and, if He had not the infirmities of man, He had not the perfections of God. For, in the same reality that He was God, He was man; for He was first begotten of the Holy Ghost, that is of God, and then He was born of the Virgin Mary, that is of a daughter of Adam, and the realities of these two facts constituted the existence of Jesus Christ; and whatever these two realities embraced, that is what He was, and as certainly embraced the imperfections of the one as the perfections of the other.

The Mother of Jesus Christ.

God being the Father of Jesus, and Mary being His mother, and God being from everlasting, and Mary not being in existence for thousands of years after the creation, and God being her Creator, how foolish the idea of Mary being the mother of God, and how foreign to all the conceptions, to all that God has placed in man, that constitutes the reasoning power, or the sense by which we discriminate between truth and error, is this preposterous idea of Mary, a daughter of Adam, being the mother of God; one who was nothing more than a fair specimen of humanity, possessing no peculiarities whatever, except that she was so highly favored of the Lord that all nations would call her blessed; one who had no other claims to greatness; one who claimed nothing more. Moreover, if she had been a being superior to man, Jesus would not have been the seed of the woman. He would not have been that prophet which was to be raised up unto them of their brethren. He would not have had our infirmities; there would be no sympathy between God and man, no High Priest who had had our infirmities and could be touched with a feeling of them. Moreover, if Mary had been in existence before the foundation of the world, and had had power to create it, the idea of her being the mother of God would be foolishness; yea, the idea is so much like the essence of folly that it seems like bringing common sense beneath its level, when we attempt to argue it. Nevertheless, Jesus Christ had a mother, and it is evident, that as man was not His father, that Mary was the mother of more than man; and though it were impossible for her to have been the mother of God, it is evident that she was the mother of all that was embraced in the union of God and man, as existing in Jesus Christ, for she was His mother, and He was God as well as man, and the God that He was, and the man that He was, was in indistinct union. But as every jot and tittle of truth teaches us that there is no separation in God, the God that Jesus was, was that which was imparted to Him by the Father, when He begat Him. And so, instead of being the mother of God, she was the mother of the union of God and man. Therefore, Mary was the mother of Jesus Christ with respect to His whole existence, for the Divine nature never had such an existence before. Thus, though Jesus was Divine, Mary, in the fullest acceptation of the term, was His mother, for that existence which He constituted never existed before. But she was no more the mother of the Divine nature, which He received from His Father, than she was the mother of her own existence; for being the mother of the being, and the mother of the nature, are two particularly distinct things, for since the beginning of creation there never was a mother that was the mother of the nature of her offspring's father.

The Union of God and Man.

There was a great object in the work of God as manifested in Jesus Christ, which seems to have been lost sight of, or at least for ages past has not been fully understood, and seems to be entirely obscured at the present day. This particular object or design of God is to be inferred or understood from the facts in the case, as existing under the two covenants. So that under the first covenant man was isolated from God, and the nature of the one was not comprehended through any sympathetic organism of the other, God being God and God only, and man being man and man only. So that that sympathetic organism which was a perquisite to the possessor of that quality, that could be touched with a feeling of our infirmity, under the old covenant, God did not possess. But, seeing its necessity from the time of fall of Adam, (for though a provision before, it was then that it became a necessity,) determined that that organism should be united with Himself. For though He could be touched with a feeling *for* our infirmities, He could not be touched with a feeling *of* them. Thus we see that under the first dispensation, God, in His dealings with man, acted through that organism in man, but without the union of that organism with Himself; thus it is that under the old dispensation, God, in His dealings with man, acted more in accordance with His justice, and less in accordance with His mercy. Hence we see the Amlikites utterly destroyed because they endeavored to destroy God's people; this, it seems, was their just deserts; and also the nations of Canaan, as nations, were destroyed because the cup of their iniquity had become full. Yet the mercy of God had been extended towards those nations until their abominations were to the full, then the just wrath of God fell upon them, unmixed with mercy, and without that mitigating effect being manifest that proceeds from a sympathetic union. And when the perfidious designs of the vile Haman were frustrated, and the Jews were rescued from that terrible slaughter that awaited them, it was not only that they escaped, but that terrible slaughter which their enemies intended for them fell, in accordance with strict justice, unmixed with mercy, upon their own heads. And when Saul was rejected he was rejected; when Uzza touched the ark he was smitten, and under the law, by the mouth of two witnesses, the man died without mercy. And though the mercy of God has been manifest in His dealings with mankind since the beginning of creation, yet the absence of that organism which alone could generate and consummate that sympathy which God desired and intended that Himself should possess, may be seen to exist under the old covenant, and its presence is clearly and unmistakably seen to exist under the new. So that under the old dispensation man was dealt with more in accordance with rigid justice, so that they learned the law in accordance with the saying, " An eye for an eye, and a tooth for a tooth." But as soon as the wonderful work of bringing about the union of God and man was consummated in the Son of God, what a change, yea, what a reverse. Judaism stunned; the sword of vengeance sheathed; the Sanhedrum, with its decrees of death, dissolved; the galling yoke broken, and the grievous burden taken away; and man lifted his head above the fading elements of the old covenant, and saw the exhibitions of rigid justice at once supplanted by the most tender manifestations of sympathetic mercy. And this glorious event has been chanted and chimed forth by men and angels, and confirmed by the audible voice of Jehovah Himself, so that even justice smiled when mercy's voice was heard.

But some say, why this change; why its necessity? Could not God have always done as He is now doing? Could not these tender dealings with mankind have been practiced always? Does not God know all things? This God Himself explains; but it is evident that those who ask the question do not know all things. For if they knew as much as Job knew, or as much as the few sentences which he gave utterance to upon this subject can teach them, they would not ask the question, but would see its great necessity, and the wonderful manifestation of God's wisdom and mercy in bringing it about. For, saith Job, when in vain he looked around him for that help which his situation called for, and realized the unapproachable greatness and dignity of the Almighty, "He is not a man as I am, that I should answer Him, and we should come together in judgment, neither is there any daysman betwixt us that might lay his hand upon us both." And who, with this before him, could fail to see the necessity of such a mediator as the Son of God, the son of man, and the wonderful manifestation of the wisdom and mercy of God in creating such a mediator as Jesus Christ, such a daysman as this, who can lay His hand upon us both. And again, in the language of the Apostle, we see the wonderful manifestation of God's wisdom and mercy in providing such a mediator, for, saith he, "In all things it behooved Christ to be made like unto His brethren," that is, that in every respect He should be made like them, and that, as a man, in no respect He should be made differently from them, "that He might be a merciful and faithful High Priest in things pertaining to God, to make reconciliation for the sins of the people, for in that He Himself hath suffered, being tempted, He is able to succor them that are tempted." And the fact that this medium of sympathy did not exist under the old covenant, being clearly shown by the language of Job, is rendered unmistakable by the fact that it was afterwards created. So that the wonderful work of God, in bringing into existence His only begotten Son, with all its other features, embraces this one particular and all-important fact, that God in so doing designed to and did unite with Himself that organism through which Himself could be in sympathy with man. Hence we see that it was as essential for Jesus Christ to be man as it was for Him to be God, and the fact that He was to be man and all that man was, and that as a man He was to be nothing more, is clearly to be seen from the nature of the case. For if as a man He had been superior to man, that organism would not have answered God's purpose; and if He had not been all that man was, then there would have been a deficiency, and the purpose of God could not have been accomplished. But as a man He was man complete; as God He was God in reality. And God and man thus united in the person Jesus Christ, His existence was no more the result of nature's creative laws, in His being the offspring of Mary, than was His existence the result of His being begotten of the Father. For the God-nature that He was, constituted His existence in the same reality as, and in indistinct union with, His humanity, so that if He was man He was God, and if He was God He was man. So that without His God-nature, the being Christ could not be, and the being Jesus Christ never was and never can be in existence without His humanity, for if the God-nature of Jesus was taken away, it would be that same God whose nature it always was, and as there is no separation in Divinity, it would be the same one God; and if the humanity or man was taken away from Him, the humanity would return to its dust, for man, according to the declaration of the Almighty who created him, is dust. So that if the

Divinity and humanity were separated, the being Jesus Christ would not be in existence; but God and man united in the being Jesus Christ, we have a Great High Priest that can be touched with a feeling of our infirmities, and through the sympathy brought about by this union God understood even the nature and terrors of death. For Christ was His Son in the nature of Himself and Mary, just as He was the Son of Mary in the nature of herself and God; and as Mary felt the pangs produced by sympathy for her Son when she beheld Him on the cross, so God felt for His Son, for He was His Son in the same reality that He was the son of Mary. Hence the consummation of the design of the Almighty, in bringing about a sympathy between Himself and mankind, is clearly seen in the union of God and man in the being Jesus Christ, whose humanity constitutes that organic structure through which God Himself can be and is in sympathy with man.

Immortality.

If there could be any immortality in man, that immortality would, of necessity, be of a Divine nature, and, of course, would be derived from God as a power of existence, and being of a Divine nature, it could be no separation from that nature. And as free agency in the present state of affairs is manifestly certain, the fact that there is no immortality in man is just as certain, for the Christian, even who has the immortal spirit within him, is nevertheless certainly mortal, both in regard to the first and second deaths, for, still having the liberty to obey or disobey, if he draw back he draws back into perdition, and is a subject for the first and the second deaths. Hence it is evident that there is no immortality in man. And the Scriptures, in regard to this matter, are very plain and pointed. As "For unto them that seek for glory, honor and immortality" is to be granted "eternal life, but tribulation and anguish upon every soul of man that doeth evil." Here we have God's promise, to the effect that if we seek for glory, honor and immortality, we shall have eternal life, which, of course, embraces glory, honor and immortality. But if we do not seek for these things, then tribulation and anguish are to be the reward, and not eternal life. Hence it is not only clear, but indisputably certain, that there is no immortality in man; and it is also clear that the immortality that is to be sought for is embraced in the eternal life, and that the eternal life is not anything that man has, but that it is to be the result of seeking for glory, honor and immortality, and this is all embraced in the obtaining of the hope of glory, which is Christ in us; for "if any man have not the spirit of Christ, he is none of His." Yea, unless He hath the spirit of Christ, the eternal spirit, which is the eternal life, there is not even a foretaste of immortality in him, for if there were immortality in man, it would be the essence of absurdity to exhort him to seek it. Hence, to maintain that there is immortality in man, is to endorse the heathen idea concerning his nature, and reject the plain and positive teachings of the Scripture to the contrary. Again, the victory over death, not only spiritual, but also literal, is to be obtained through Jesus, as saith the Apostle, "Thanks be to God, who giveth us the victory, through our Lord Jesus Christ." And this victory, which is brought about through Him, is to be completed when this corruptible shall have put on incorruption, and this mortal shall have put on immortality, for it is then that death is to be swallowed up in victory (and how absurd the idea that death is to bring about this victory), and so this victory is to be completed when those who have the immortal spirit, the spirit of Jesus Christ, within them, which is to quicken or change them from corruptible to incorruptible, and from mortal to immortal, are to be the recipients of this change, and are not only to have the witness of the spirit within them, but are to be clothed with immortality, or to be that which they were not before, immortal beings. Hence, how conspicuous the fact that there is no immortality in man. And as regards the nature or existence of man in this and the future states, that existence is to be realized and embraced by the one and the same being, and is to embrace the one and the same being in the future state that it does in this, and that being is man's own self. And man is that being whom God made of the dust of the ground, and into whose nostrils He breathed the breath of life, and who then became a living soul. Not that he became a different being from what he was before, but the man being of the earth earthy, he was an inanimate being whom God had made with His hands, and thus made, he was all that is embraced in the word man. And then God breathed into his nostrils the breath of life, and thus man became a living soul. Hence we see that man is the being which God thus created, and this being is the one referred to when man is mentioned, just as Job meant when referring to this being, or speaking of man, thus, "Thou wilt have a desire to the work of thy hands." So we see that first the man was made, and that then he received the breath of life; therefore it is clear, that as man was the recipient of the breath of life, that he was man complete before he received it; and it is just as positive that he was man the same, or the same man after he was deprived of it, that is because he was man at first without it, and then became a living soul with it; and then being deprived of it, he was the same man that he was before he received it. And it is evident, that without this breath of life which God breathed into man, by which he became a living soul, he could not exist. And it is evident that the eternal life is the only immortality, and that Christ is the way and the life; that His humanity is the way and His Divinity is the life; that His humanity, as embraced in the natural life is the way, and that His Divinity is the eternal life. And this life eternal, or eternal life, is made more comprehensible by the language of Paul, who, when speaking of the present and future natures of man, he says: "It is sown a natural body; it is raised a spiritual body." That is, the natural body, when it is raised, will be raised a spiritual body. For the natural life ceases when the blood ceases to flow through the body, for the blood is the life that is of the body, which is the natural body, and when this life has ceased from it, then it is sown a natural body; but when this natural body is raised, it is raised a spiritual body; not that it is raised what is termed spiritually, or that it is a spirit, but this body which is sown or buried a natural body, which body, prior to its being sown, was sustained by the blood, which was its life, is to be raised destitute of that blood or natural life which it once had, and which ceased, and is to be raised by the spirit which dwelt in it, which spirit, instead of its blood, is to be its life, and thus quickened or made alive, or made to live again through the quickening power of the Spirit of God, it will be a spiritual body, the life of which is to be that spirit, the eternal spirit which is to be its eternal life.

When Jesus was on earth He was a mortal being, but after His resurrection He was an immortal being; and when He permitted His followers to see Him after His resurrection, the evidence that He gave of Himself was that He was not a spirit, but flesh and bones. And whatever Jesus was as regards the natural body and the natural life, the death or change of the body and life, and its existence here and hereafter, the same is true concerning His saints. For as Jesus was man and natural, so are His disciples, and as Jesus died and thus yielded up the natural life, His blood, the natural life being shed upon the cross, so His followers are subject to the same natural death or termination of the natural life. And as when Jesus had given up the Ghost, and His natural existence had ceased, and He, the same person, was laid in the tomb, so His saints, after they have ended their natural lives, are laid in their graves; and as Jesus, the same person who died on the cross and was laid in the tomb, whose natural life had ceased, was raised from the dead, that is, was quickened, made alive or made to live, so His saints, who are laid in the tomb, are to be quickened, made alive or made to live; that is, they themselves, not the shadows of them, for their natural bodies are to be raised, just as the natural body of their Lord was raised, the difference being that He was not suffered to see corruption. And as when His natural body was raised, it was raised a spiritual body, and afterwards became a glorious body, so are the natural bodies of His saints to be raised spiritual bodies, and then to become glorious bodies. For Christ is to "change our vile body, that it may be fashioned like unto His glorious body, according to the working whereby He is able even to subdue all things unto Himself."

Faith.

"Faith is the substance of things hoped for, the evidence of things not seen."

There is nothing more inconsistent with the fact that we are free agents than the idea that faith is a special gift. For if it were a special gift, this special gift would be the great prerequisite to all that is embraced in Christianity. And as in the absence of it this faith is to be obtained by him who obtains it without faith, and his nature being exactly at variance with it, and this faith teaching him that without faith it is impossible to please Him who is the giver of this faith, it is evident that the effort to obtain it would never be made. And as it embraces the idea that God requires that man, in his efforts to obtain His favor, should first make use of that which he has not, and that without that which he has not he cannot obtain that which he must have, it is evident that the idea that faith is a special gift is altogether erroneous. On the other hand, it embraces the idea that as man is destitute of this faith, and that it is a special gift and a positive necessity, or the great essential to salvation, that for God to be just He should first bestow this gift. And this would make salvation the gift of God to those whom He might choose, and this without effort or will on their part, or the least discrimination between right and wrong. In fact, it would make them mere machines, instead of responsible beings, and those who did not receive the gift would certainly be free from responsibility. In fact, it is the essence of folly to attempt to sustain the notion that faith is a special gift. The idea itself seems like the production of drowsy stupidity. For through this particular faith we are saved by grace, and this particular faith must precede the grace by which we are saved. "For by grace are ye saved through faith; and that not of yourselves: it is the gift of God;" that is, the grace which is received through faith is the gift. For grace and truth came by Jesus Christ, but faith did not come by Him, for it is that inherent principle of our nature through which we are to receive the grace by which we are to be saved. For the grace is a free gift, and "the gift of God is eternal life through Jesus Christ, our Lord." But the grace, or eternal life, which is the gift, is received through faith, for faith is belief, and is just as applicable in any other sense as in a Christian sense, even if that faith is nothing more than a contradiction of the Christian faith. For when a man believes that Christ was the son of Joseph or some other man, and that the prophecies concerning His first advent and the claims of Christ to fulfill them, and the teachings of the Apostles concerning Him, amount to nothing but superstition and cunningly devised fables, and that Christ was an imposter, this is his faith or belief, and this his free agency gives him the privilege of doing. But when a man believes that Jesus Christ was the Son of God, that He fulfilled the prophecies concerning Him, and thus proved that He was the Messiah; when he believes the teachings of Christ and places his hope of salvation on the atoning blood and merits of Jesus, then he has the faith of Christ, faith in Christ, and this is his faith. And this faith, in either case, is the result of the operations of the mind, subject more or less to the powers which constitute the will, and is, in the abstract, the same in substance, and is an inherency of his nature, which moves or operates in union with or in opposition to his will, as embraced in the fact that he is a free agent. And it is no special gift, but a power alike possessed by all men, and is the result of the action of the brain in discriminating between truth and error. This discrimination, however, may, by submission to the baser principles of nature, become deranged, so that the power of discrimination may be governed more by the rulings of the passions than by the equally balanced or unbiased operations of the mind.

Predestination.

This belief, or rather the manner in which it is believed by those who are termed Predestinationists, in its most extensive sense, embraces some of the most extravagant ideas, and has called forth some of the most blasphemous assertions, with respect to the attributes of the Almighty, that it is possible to conceive of as being the productions of an evil heart, much less the teachings of intelligent and well-meaning men. And hence such a faith, or the pretensions of such a faith, no matter in whom or where manifest, should be regarded as the offspring of heathenism in its origin, and the most bigoted credulity in those who receive it. For those who teach or have taught what they call predestination, teach that before man was created God first contemplated and then determined that He would create man, and that he should not be a free agent, but that, whether he would or no, he should be forced into sin: and that he and all his offspring should alike become criminals in His sight; and that then He would bring about things in such a manner as to accomplish the sacrifice of His only begotten Son in behalf of some of these criminals. Not because they repented of their sins and forsook them, or because they believed on His Son (though they might have done both), but because He had chosen them before they were created: that is, because He had created them for that purpose, and inasmuch as they were predestinated to be saved, they could not be lost. And that all others were created by the foreknowledge of God for the purpose of finally being damned, or, rather, that they were damned before they were created, and then created to be punished; and that no matter how penitent they were, how much they implored the mercy of the Almighty, no matter how much they believed on His Son, He had consigned them to an eternal hell before they were created, and to hell they must go. And dark as this picture is, it is far from being its blackest color; for this doctrine robs Satan of his attributes and attributes them to the Almighty, for it represents God as being as bad as Satan would be if he could, and worse than he could be if he would. But this is no more in accordance with the attributes of the Divine Being than the devouring of an infant by a wild beast is in accordance with the tender love of its mother. Hence, if those who choose to believe such diabolical teachings concerning the Deity, had chosen Satan for their God, they would have acted more consistently, and been free from this terrible scandal against the Almighty. Therefore, the proper disposition to be made of these teachings is to class them with the damnable heresies that were to be brought into the church.

Among the passages of Scripture adduced to sustain the abominable notion of predestination, as presented above, the following are the most conspicuous: "The Lord made all things for Himself. He made the wicked for the day of evil." True, but He did not make the wicked do wickedly; but, after they became wicked and remained in their wickedness, then He consigned them to the day of evil, or the punishment of that day, for "the wicked are to be turned into hell, and all the nations that forget God."

Again: "I make peace and create evil." That is, He checks the violence of the wicked, and brings evil upon the workers of iniquity, as is taught everywhere; but He does not create the evil works of the wicked, for such are their works, not His.

"O Lord, I know that the way of a man is not in himself." This is construed to imply that no matter what way a man goes, that is the way he is forced to go, and he can go no other; whereas, the text teaches that the way he should go, or the right way, is not in himself, for the carnal mind is enmity against God, and cannot be brought into that way without Divine assistance, which it can always have, and is sure to have; for Christ, being the light that lighteneth every man that cometh into the world, through that light or enlightening He presents Himself to the man as the living and true way, and shows him that His way, or the right way, is not in himself, but that He is the way and the life.

"For we know that all things work together for good to them that love God, to them who are called according to His purpose." That is, according to

His purpose as He purposed in Christ Jesus, before the foundation of the world.

"For whom He did foreknow, He also did predestinate to be conformed to the image of His Son." As Christ was foreordained to be their Saviour, if they would accept Him, so they were predestined to be conformed to His image.

"Elect according to the foreknowledge of God the Father, through sanctification of the Spirit unto obedience and sprinkling of the blood of Christ." This, instead of teaching that man is predestined to be saved or to be damned, is in perfect harmony with the plan of salvation as embracing his free agency. For God foreknew and determined that man should be a free agent, and that if he chose evil instead of good, that through sanctification of the Spirit, or the work of the Spirit, and the sprinkling of the blood of Jesus Christ, He would bring about his salvation, notwithstanding his fall; and so this obedience, which would be of faith, would be accepted as a substitute for the other. Hence, they were elect according to the foreknowledge of God the Father, just as Jesus Christ, His Son, was foreordained according to the same foreknowledge, and with their own free will were excepted through the provision made by the foreordaining of Christ, or by their complying with the terms of the provision which this foreordaining constituted. Hence we see that, instead of God foreordaining man to eternal damnation, and fixing his destiny so that over it he could not have the least control, he was not only created with the inherency of self will or free agency, but, even before he was created, there was a provision made for him in case he should fail to use his liberty in accordance with the will of the Almighty who created him with this dignifying attribute; and that, notwithstanding his fall, this free will or agency stands forth as a manifest feature of the plan of salvation; and that this free agency is that which the whole fabric is founded upon, without which the Bible, instead of being the Word of the living and true God, would be but a scandal against Him.

Mystery.

"Now to Him who is of power to establish you according to my Gospel, and the preaching of Jesus Christ, according to the revelation of the mystery, which was kept secret since the world began, But now is made manifest, and by the Scriptures of the Prophets, according to the commandment of the everlasting God, made known to all nations for the obedience of faith."—*Romans, XVI ch., 25th and 26th vs.* Here we see that the preaching of Jesus was not according to any mystery, but according to the revelation of the mystery which from the beginning of the world to that time had been kept secret. But now, says the Apostle, "is made manifest, and by the Scriptures of the Prophets, according to the commandment of the everlasting God, made known to all nations for the obedience of faith." That is, this which was kept secret, which secret constituted the mystery which had been made *manifest* by the Scriptures of the Prophets, according to the commandment of the everlasting God, *was then made known*, not to a few persons to transmit to others as private knowledge, but to all nations, or all the world, for the obedience of faith, not in a mystery, but in this revelation of the mystery; that is, that Christ came into the world to save both Jew and

Gentile, or all sinners. That fallen man required a substitute, and that Christ was an all-sufficient sacrifice; that through Him alone is redemption; that there is no other name given under heaven whereby we are to be saved but the name of Jesus Christ, of Nazareth, who died for our sins and rose again for our justification; who ascended into heaven, and now, as our intercessor, sitteth at the right hand of God; from thence expecting or waiting till His foes be made His footstool. This is what was made manifest by the Scriptures of the Prophets, and, according to the commandment of the everlasting God, was then made known to all nations, for them to believe, embrace and live, according to I Corinthians, chapter II, 7th verse: "But we speak the wisdom of God in a mystery, even the hidden wisdom which God ordained before the world unto our glory." Here, in this verse, we see that the mystery spoken of is the knowledge that the Christian has, and concerning which he can teach; which knowledge is the result of experience, or is the experience of the Christian, and which constitutes the difference between the knowledge that the worldling can have and that which the Christian possesses, as shown in the next verse, for says he, it is that wisdom "which none of the princes of this world knew." And hence it is that which the Christian knows, that those of the world do not know, and this which the Christian alone knows, is the reality of the Divine presence of Jesus Christ, or Christ in him the hope of glory. Hence, if the princes of this world had understood this wisdom, which is the perfection of the believer, they would not have crucified the Lord of Glory, but would have gloried in Him as their Lord. But those who have not the spirit do not understand the intrinsical reality of Christianity; to them this innateness is a mystery. But when they are converted and receive the Holy Spirit, then there is no more mystery, because it is all revealed unto them. Ephesians, III ch., 3d verse: "How that by revelation He made known unto me the mystery; as I wrote afore in few words." Here we see that as the mystery was revealed unto him so he revealed it unto them, though in few words. Fourth verse: "Whereby when ye read ye may understand my knowledge in the mystery of Christ." Here we see that if he had not revealed the mystery unto them they would not have understood his knowledge of it, for they would not have been foolish enough to believe that such a one as Paul understood the Gospel, because he told them that he understood a mystery. Fifth verse: "Which in other ages was not made known unto the sons of men, as it is now revealed unto His holy Apostles and Prophets by the Spirit." And what is it that was not made known unto the sons of men in other ages? Why just that which is revealed in the next verse, "That the Gentiles should be fellow-heirs, and of the same body, and partakers of His promise in Christ by the Gospel." Ephesians, chapter I, 9th verse: "Having made known unto us the mystery of His will, according to His good pleasure which He hath purposed in Himself." Here we see that God made known the mystery of His will. But to accord with the teachings of those who talk about a glorious mystery, and those who hold that they are teachers of the mystery, and that they alone are to be heard concerning it, it would be necessary for this verse to read thus: That God has made known the fact that His will is a mystery. But, to the contrary of this, not only do we see that God has made known unto us His will, but that He was pleased to do so; that it was a pleasure to God to wipe out all mystery, and make plain to all men His will concerning them.

The Word.

If Christ was not at the right hand of God we should have no intercessor. If Christ had not risen from the dead there would have been no justification. If Christ had not died there would have been no atonement. If Christ had not preached and practiced there would have been no Gospel. If Christ had not been born there would have been no Saviour; neither would that prophet have been raised up unto them of their brethren, like unto Moses, and neither would the Child, the Son, the Wonderful, the Counsellor, the Mighty God, the Everlasting Father, the Prince of Peace, have been. And now let those who entertain the idea that Christ existed before He was born of the Virgin Mary, endeavor to ascertain which of these assertions are false; but if they all prove correct, then let them endeavor to find out what there would have been of Jesus Christ, if all this which has been spoken of had not come to pass. For if there be any sense in language, the one who was born of the Virgin Mary fulfilled all these characters. Yet, when He is divested of His birth, and all that followed it, they might say that He was the Word, for "the Word was made flesh and dwelt among us." Yea, the Word was made flesh, or to exist in the flesh, and, as has been said before, this Word was the Divine nature of Jesus, which was imparted to Him by the Father, when He begat Him, and this nature was not only the Word of God (for that was then its name), but it was God. Yea, it could not have been other than God, and was the same that was in the beginning, for that which was called the Word was God in Christ, and that Word was what was in the beginning with God, and was God. Not that the Word was the Word in the beginning, but that which was then the Word was in the beginning. So that John, in referring to the Word, did not mean that Christ, as the Word, was in the beginning, but that the Divinity of Christ, which was then the Word, was in the beginning with God, and was God, apart of Himself. Hence the glory of the Word, or the Word's glory, was seen after He was begotten of the Father, but not before, for when they beheld it, it was as the glory of the only begotten of the Father, but before it was not His glory, for His Divine nature was with God, and was God, and there was no God but the Father.

The Valley of Dry Bones.

"The hand of the Lord was upon me, and carried me out in the Spirit of the Lord, and set me down in the midst of the valley, which was full of bones. And caused me to pass by them round about; and behold, there were very many in the open valley; and lo, they were very dry."—*Ezekiel, XXXVII ch.* Here the prophet was permitted the most meagre view possible of that which was to be presented to his mind, whereby he was to get an understanding of the reality of the case with respect to all the house of Israel. This was simply a starting point, to show to the prophet what was to be the future of those whose condition was thus represented; and thus the most that the prophet could make of them was that they were bones which were very dry, and then, continuing, he says: "And He said unto me, Son of man, can these bones live?" Here the prophet failed to declare the fact, and left it to the Lord to answer the question. And how did He answer it? Why, just as He alone was capable of doing it, as says the prophet: "Again He said unto me, prophesy upon these bones, and say unto them, O, ye dry bones, hear the Word of God. Thus saith the Lord God unto these bones: behold, I will cause breath to enter into you, and ye shall live."

Here, though there is but the bones of men, and they dry, yea, very dry, God says unto them: I will cause breath to enter into you, and ye shall live. Here God presents before us just enough of the reality of man to allow us to understand what He is going to do, and upon whom it is to be done, and then says He, "I will lay sinews upon you." Here we have the work of reconstruction fairly began: the bones, which were very dry, with sinews upon them. And who were they? What were they? They were the whole house of Israel. And so the work of reconstruction goes on, for, says He, "I will bring up flesh upon you, and cover you with skin." Here is the regular course of reconstruction: the last that remains is the first restored. First, the framework, then the sinews, then the flesh, and then the covering of skin; and then says the Lord, I will "put breath into you." What breath? Surely the breath of life, for, says He, "And ye shall *live.*" And again, says He, "And ye shall know that I am the Lord." Did not they know it always? No. "The dead know not anything." Through all this there is not so much as a shadow of such an idea as that the house of Israel, or any of it, was alive in heaven, for, says He, "These are the whole house of Israel." Yea, those dry bones represented the whole house of Israel. But what a picture to represent the glorious reality of the songs of praise, the unspeakable rejoicing, the everlasting felicity that, according to the heretical teachings of the present age, are the reality of the situation of the righteous of the house of Israel, not where there are such things as dry bones, but in heaven, and even before the throne itself. Alas for their hope. But thus it is that the fabulous teachings of the present day, and that of the Sacred Volume, differ. The fabulous teach that heaven is the place of reward, and that death is the gateway thither. But God carries the prophet's vision down to the Valley of Dry Bones, and gives him a clear view of them, and shows him that death is the gateway thither, and that there is where the whole house of Israel is. Hence, the difference between fallacy and truth is the difference between the most of the teachings of the present day and the picture which, in this chapter, is presented before us. And when the prophet again prophesied, he saw the fulfillment of all that was spoken concerning them. He saw that as man was created at the first, that so these were re-created, but that there was no breath in them, just as there was no breath in Adam; and then he saw that breath came into them. Here the prophet had presented before him the whole process of reconstruction or re-creation, beginning at the bones, until the whole man was completed, and then the call was made. But where? Not to heaven, for those imaginary beings to return to their earthly tenements, from which they had been so long and happily separated, but the call was from the four winds: " Come from the four winds, O, breath, and breathe upon these slain, that they may live." Here the work was completed, the man was re-created just as He was at the first created, and the breath of life animated their organisms the same as it did that of Adam; and then says the prophet: "They lived and stood upon their feet, an exceeding great army." Here the difference between the reality of the nature of man and the heretical teachings concerning his being of an immortal nature is clearly manifested, for the man was re-created as he was first created, and re-animated as he was first animated, and in both cases the organic structure and the breath of life were what and all that constituted his existence. But when is all this to transpire? When? Why just when the Lord said it should, for says He unto the prophet, "Son of man, these bones are the whole house of Israel: behold, they say, our bones are dried, and our hope is lost: we are cut off from our parts. (But the present-day believers tell us that at death they just enter upon that from which these were cut off.) Therefore prophesy and say unto them, Thus saith the Lord God; behold, O my people, I will open your graves, and cause you to come up out of your graves, and bring you unto the land of Israel. And ye shall know that I am the Lord, when I have opened your graves, O my people, and brought you up out of your graves, And shall put my spirit in you, and ye shall live, and I shall put you in your own land: then shall ye know that I the Lord have spoken it, and performed it, saith the Lord." Was it when He called them from heaven? was it when He declared that the immortal beings which existed in the felicitous regions of eternal glory, who had escaped from this sin-cursed earth through the Divine blessing of death, should return to their earthly abode and again occupy those dusty shells which He had again created? Alas for such ideas. But why not entertain them, for they would be but the reality of the teachings of the present day? But mark the difference between this and the reality of God's Word, for says He: "I will open your graves and cause you to come up out of your graves." And who was this *I?* Was it God? And who was this *you?* Was it God's people? Yea, *I* was God, and *you* was His people. Therefore, as this *I* was God, who brought them out of their graves, and this *I* was He Himself, *you* was the people themselves. If *I* were God, who thus re-created them, just as surely *you* were those who were thus re-created. Hence, this *I* was God's own self, and this *you* was their own selves. It was no one but God who re-created, it was none but those who were dead who were re-created. This not only shows the process of re-creation, but plainly presents the fact that re-creation is necessary, in order that these may again exist, and hence shows that they do not and will not exist until that re-creation takes place, and that when the organic structure is again brought into existence, and the breath of life breathed into it, that then it will be all that it ever was, and that that all is necessary to constitute its existence, and that prior to that time these souls will not exist.

The Resurrection.

As God made man of the dust of the ground, and that man returned to dust again, it would be no more trouble for God to resurrect or re-create that identical man of some other dust than it would be for Him to re-create him of that particular dust to which he had returned. For he was made of the dust of the ground, and not any particular dust, except that particular part of the dust which he constituted, or, rather, that constituted him. So that as the man was made of dust and returned to dust, the dust that he was and the dust to which he returned were identical, one and the same dust, the same as and with all other dust. And it was not because he was dust that he was man, but because of the making or the being made, or the being that he was after he was made. Hence if God had left that particular dust of which Adam was first made undisturbed where it was, and had taken a parcel of dust from another place and made him in like manner, this would not have changed the case with respect to Adam. No, there would not have been the least shadow of difference. So then, as Adam was made of the dust of the ground and returned to that particular dust again, if that particular dust had been deposited exactly where it had been taken from, then the dust of the ground would have been just as it was before the man was made, and just as though he never had been made, and the man would not be in existence, for the existence of the dust of the ground does not constitute his existence. So that if at the resurrection or re-creation, God should take that particular dust which we supposed Him not to take at the first, and of which Adam was first made, and should make him or raise him to life again as he was when he was first made, the particular dust of which he was made would make no difference to his case whatever, but he would be the same, the identical being, for the dust of the ground was not the man, but the being that was made of the dust was the man. Therefore it is not the dust but the making that constitutes the man, for one parcel of dust is the same as another parcel of dust, and the first parcel is the same as the last; and as both parcels are dust and nothing but dust, it would not matter of which parcel Adam was made or to which parcel he returned, or of which parcel he was resurrected or re-created, for it is all one and the same one dust. Therefore we may not wonder at the language of Job, when he says, " As the waters fail from the sea, and the flood decayeth and drieth up; So man lieth down, and riseth not: till the heavens be no more, they shall not awake, nor be raised out of their sleep." Thus we see that man, unlike the tree that is cut down, does not yield a germ or shoot that will spring into existence; but as the flood decayeth and drieth up, so man lieth down and riseth not. And why does he not rise? why does not that shoot come forth? Why, because he is not as the tree that is cut down, but as the flood that decayeth and drieth up. And as the flood, when it is decayed and dried up, is not, does not exist, so man, when he lieth down and returneth to his dust, is not; for if otherwise Job would not have declared him to be as the flood instead of as the tree. But he knew that he was dust, and that unto dust he should return, and seeing that the workmanship of his being was to be dissolved, that he was to pass away, and that he was to be as though he had not been, he exclaims, "If a man die, shall he live again?" and then, as though he had received an answer direct from the Almighty, he says, "all the days of my appointed time will I wait till my change come," and then, with all the confidence that that answer could excite, he says, "Thou shalt call and I will answer Thee; Thou wilt have a desire to the works of Thine hands," not to the dust to which he was to return, but to that workmanship of the Almighty which he saw was to be dissolved. And then continues, "For I know that my Redeemer liveth, and that He shall stand at the latter day upon the earth: And though after my skin worms destroy this body, yet in my flesh shall I see God: Whom I shall see for myself, and mine eye shall behold, and not another; though my veins be consumed within me." This is equivalent to saying, that though I return to the dust of the ground and the workmanship that I am shall have vanished away, and though it be with me as though I had not been, yet, when the hand that made me and fashioned me brings me forth again, it will not be another Job, but I myself, who will see God. For it was the workmanship which Job referred to, and not the dust of which he was made and to which he was to return. So the resurrection of the dead, the wonderful manifestation of the power of God in bringing into existence those who have passed away, of bringing about that change which alone could satisfy David; the fruition of that hope for which Paul was bound with chains; the realizing of that to which Abraham looked when he was about to offer up Isaac; of that which was the only comfort of the afflicted Job; of that to which Christ and His Apostles pointed with so much precision; that which ramifies the whole organization of Christianity, and without which it would vanish into nothingness; that wonderful work that is to be accomplished has not been placed on record to be received and believed simply because Omnipotence is not limited in power. But, notwithstanding the scavelings and squirmings of skeptics and scorners, and the mystifiers of the Scripture and the would-be expounders of the Word, the wonderful work of resurrecting the dead is not only known to Omniscience, but it hath pleased the Almighty to reveal it in His Holy Word, as practicable in the sight of man.

The Mind is not the Spirit, but the Mind is the Brain.

It is evident, according to the organization of man and the teachings of the Scriptures, that there is nothing to induce the belief that the mind is the spirit; neither that it is possible that the operations of the mind or the reasoning faculty is, or is a part of what is, in reality the spirit. For a man may lose his reason in part, or he may be wholly deprived of it, or he may not have possessed it except in part, or he may not have possessed it at all, yet he would be a man, and, hence, the possessor of a spirit; for there is a spirit in man. And if there be a spirit in man, notwithstanding the fact that he may have lost his reason, or that he may never have possessed it, it is evident that the spirit is not the mind or the reasoning power, or else when the reason was gone the spirit would be gone. Moreover, the Scriptures, in pointing to this subject, are very plain, and show clearly that the separation of the spirit from the body means death. For when Jesus raised the damsel, her spirit came again, and she lived, thus showing that at death her spirit departed, and that without her spirit she was dead. Again, the fact that faith without works is dead, is shown from the fact that the body without the spirit is dead. And again, when viewing the subject in connection with the realities of nature, as each must necessarily realize them, we see that when the mind produces a thought, and that thought is thrown out by the voice and wounds the feelings of another, that that thought is no more the mind than a stone thrown from the same person's hand would be his hand. For the hand gets the stone from somewhere, and the mind gets the thought from somewhere, and as the hand uses the arm and casts the stone, so the mind uses the voice and casts the thought; and hence we see in this a cause and an effect, neither of which, it will be seen, can be the spirit. Moreover, the mind is something that the man has always, and which is required to act, to do service, and the thoughts that it produces are simply the result of that action. And the mind cannot generate or produce without first gathering the materials for that production, any more than a grist mill can produce flour without grain; and it would be just as consistent to say that a barrel of flour was a grist mill, as it would be to say that the ideas or thoughts that the mind produces are the mind. Hence it is evident that the mind of man is not what many suppose it to be—the spirit of man—but that it is that acting or producing power; that it is the brain, that literal organ which constitutes such a prominent part of the physical organization; for that which is termed the mental part is only the result of the action of the physical organism, *the one being the cause and the other being simply the effect*. For if the mind were something outside of the physical organism, it would be supernatural, and could comprehend that which was not natural, or that did not belong to nature. But, instead of this, the comprehension of man is confined to a physical existence, or this present state of things; and hence we see that men are differently informed and capable of different things, according to the different circumstances in which they have been placed. For it is not for a farmer to describe the scenes of the ocean, or for a sailor to teach agriculture, and the reason why their minds do not produce in these respective ways, is because their brains have not gathered, or had the opportunity to gather, the materials for such production. But each having gathered according to the position he has occupied, the brain is capable of producing such ideas as constitute a description of that for which it has had the opportunity of gathering the materials. Hence, all the originality that there is in the productions of the brain, is that which is the result of combination, and that which is drawn or taken from that which already exists; and therefore the mind must first gather, and then produce, as, when a man thinks he ought to do a certain thing, the mind does not produce that thought until it has first gathered the materials, which materials are the facts that exist as a reason why that thing should be done. But in the absence of or aside from the brain, there is no such thing as gathering or producing. A man may lose either his arms, his legs, his ears, his eyes, his nose, or his speech, and yet his mind may be uninjured. But touch his brain, and the mind swerves, and as it degenerates, all manifestations that denote the presence of the mind are enfeebled until the brain is incapable of gathering, and its productions cease and then that which is termed the mind is gone. Hence it is evident that the mind is not the spirit, and it is just as evident that it is not a combination of effects, which most certainly establishes the fact that it is the brain. And as this thing, or no thing, that is called the mind cannot maintain its equilibrium with the least defect or derangement of the brain, it is manifestly certain that, instead of its being a cause, it is simply an effect, and that the brain, being the producing power, is the only reality of mind, and that there is no power that controls or even affects it, except as it is affected by or through the powers of the physical organism, with which it is in perfect harmony, and of which it forms such a conspicuous part. And how unreasonable to say that the brain is not the mind, while all are forced to admit that there cannot be a single idea produced without the action of the brain, and that if the brain is deranged there cannot be produced a single reliable thought. Again, if you wish to determine as to whether the mind is something independent of the physical organism, something which the brain is not, cut the nerves that connect the eyes with the brain and you have a blind mind. Close the ears and you have a deaf mind; destroy the speech and you have a dumb mind, for this thing called the mind, being simply effect, can only exist in proportion to the causes which are the functions of the whole man. And in proportion as these are absent, so this so-called mind is absent; as when a man is deaf, dumb and blind, there are three prominent defects in the physical organism, and this thing called the mind is a failure just so far as these defects exist, else it would manifest itself independent of them. Hence this thing called the mind is diminished three parts of the whole by the absence of these essential organs. Then destroy the smell and taste, and five parts are absent, and all just in proportion to the defects in the physical organism. Then destroy the feeling, which can be produced in any part of the physical organism, and the last shadow of the so-called mind disappears. Hence, when all these parts are removed, there is nothing left but the natural materials which constituted the physical structure; and hence, the cause being absent, there is no effect. But if all these parts were re-united and put in full healthy action, each moving in harmony with the other, they would be the physical parts of the physical structure, and these physical parts would constitute the same organism that the absence of each part made deficient in proportion to its absence. Hence, when all these parts were combined and put in action, whatever was the result of that action would necessarily be an effect, the cause of which would be their action. Hence, it is evident that outside or aside from the brain and its kindred physical auxiliaries, there is no such thing as mind, as the Psalmist, 146th, has plainly shown us when he said: "His breath goeth forth, he returneth to his earth, in that very day his thoughts perish."

A Few Sketches of the Mind, as Presented by the Physiologist, or the Physiologist and the Mind.

And, as it might be supposed that the physiologist is the proper person to define the mind, it will be well to keep in view the fact that all his operations are confined to the physical organism, and that instead of developing what is called the mind, He in reality only develops the wonderful powers of the physical organism. Hence, says an eminent physiologist, " the mind may be defined as that something which thinks, feels, and causes voluntary motion, and belongs only to man." And then, as if he were determined to have a mind somewhere outside of the reality of things, he adds: " True, the honey-comb of the bee is constructed with all the precision of consummate art. The fox crosses and recrosses his track, that he may mislead the hounds. The horse neighs when he approaches his old home, showing how joyfully he remembers the place. Still more like exalted humanity, the faithful dog grieves over the decease of his master, loses his appetite, pines away, and dies. ·Yet all this is not mental action. It is but the effect of instinct." And then he might well have added, that here his folly was manifest; for, says he, consummate art, the most sagacious manifestations, the remembering or calling to mind of that which has passed, the knowledge of loss, and sensitive grief, are not mental action. Here he shows the reality of mental action, and then denies the existence of that which he has just described, and thereby shows how little he knows of the mind. And so all his efforts to define the mind terminate only in establishing the fact that the brain, and nothing else, is the mind, as will be clearly seen by the following. For, says he: "The fact that the brain is used when the mind feels, is certain from the fact that when a person is stunned, or the brain is affected in various other ways, no feeling is or can be produced." Here he has disposed of his imaginary mind, and frankly confessed that the brain is the mind. And then he adds, that "How the mind uses the brain, is not known." Very true; and it is evident from the foregoing that it never will be known. Again, says he: "That the mind uses the nerves in the act of feeling, is certain from the effects of injury; thus, a young lady, falling on a piece of glass, cut off the nerve at the middle of the elbow, and has not felt anything since with the little finger or the adjoining part of the next finger, in which part the nerve commences." This is quite reasonable, for its communication with the brain was cut off, and hence no feeling was communicated to the brain. But why did not the so-called mind make it feel, and let it know that the brain had not all to say about feeling. And again, says he: "The organs of sense is the name given to those parts of the body in which the nerves of sensation commence. They are those parts through which, or by means of which, the nerves are acted on. They differ from each other on account of the difference in the nature of the things which are designed to act on the nerves through them. The eye is adapted to be acted upon by what is called light, and by means of which things are seen. The ear is adapted to be acted upon by waves of air, by means of which sounds are heard. The nose is adapted to be acted upon by odors, and a person can smell. The mouth is adapted to be acted upon by the savory properties of bodies, and thus a person tastes. When an object is warmer or colder than the skin, the nerves commencing in it will be acted on, as they will be, also, by the pressure of anything, and the mind learns the presence, temperature, hardness, etc., of an object." Hence, it is evident that as the mind learns these things by the application of them to the physical parts, that the realizing of them is through the physical part or parts acted upon; and as the brain is the only one organ which, by its auxiliaries or the branchings forth of itself, ramifies the whole organism, it is evident that the brain receives its information at the point acted upon, and that it, and nothing else, communicates the feeling or sensation to the whole being. Again, says he: "There are six kinds of organs of sense used in feeling, or, in other words, to *gather all the knowledge we possess of all the things in creation around us.* For what knowledge of a thing does a man possess that he does not acquire by seeing, hearing, smelling, tasting, touching, or pressing it? (Mark it, reader, what has he done with his so-called mind?) The manner in which a person feels is this, some object acts upon or through some organ of sense, thereby an effect is produced upon the nerve commencing in the organ of sense, and extending to the brain through the nerve, an effect is produced on or through the brain." This teaches so plainly that the brain is the mind, that when we look at it soberly it looks as if the author's brain turned when he adds " that thereby an effect is produced on the mind." Again, says he: " Five things are therefore necessary to produce a feeling or sensation in the ordinary way: first, an object; second, an organ of sense; third, a nerve; fourth, the brain; fifth, the mind," and then adds the following inference: " The kind of sensation will therefore depend upon the action of the object, the state of the organ of sense, the nerves, the brain, and the mind; and, that the sensation may be natural and the knowledge correct, it is necessary that all parts of the body mentioned be healthy." Here the physical organism is placed on its own account, and made responsible for every, even the slightest, deviation of the mind; so that the eye is not to be depended upon unless it is healthy. A defect in the nerve forms an obstruction between the visual organ and the brain, and, in fine, the mind, as he terms it, must have everything in the physical organism perfect, that everything may be done perfectly; and then, that which is done is all that he has to constitute that mind. Hence, it is evident that that which he calls the mind, instead of being cause, is simply effect, and, therefore, according to the realities of the case, he is correct. For effect will necessarily have the perfection or imperfection of the cause. Again, says he: "There are two kinds of nerves, one of which may be said to commence in the various parts of the body and extend to the brain; the other commencing at the brain and extending into every part of the body; for the action through one kind of nerves takes place towards the brain; through the other, from the brain." Here we may say with propriety, that this author, though endeavoring to establish the visionary mind, nevertheless plainly pictures before us the brain as enthroned and monarch of the whole organization, in communication with every part, even to the foundation of a single hair, and master of every movement. Again says he: "The mind causes the muscles to contract or relax by, in the first place, causing the brain to produce nervous influence; in the second place, causing it to act upon the muscles, by the contraction and relaxation of which a desired motion can be produced." And then, says he: "In the production of voluntary motion it is the duty of the brain, at the wish of the mind, to produce nervous influence; it is the duty of the nerves to transmit the influence to the muscles; the duty of the muscles to contract or relax the instant they receive the influence which impels them to the one or the other." And then, adds the inference: "Since the speech, expression of face, gesticulation, and everything by which the mind communicates its ideas, exhibits its emotions, or acts upon the world, depends upon the actions of the muscles; and, since these are controlled by the brain and nerves, it is essential to efficient action or expression that the muscles, brain and nerves be preserved in health." Here he tells us that at the wish of the mind, the brain does certain things, and then tells us that the perfection of an *effect* will depend upon the perfection of the *cause*, thus, making the physical organism responsible as the *cause* and the *effect* denoting the condition of the cause, and concentrating everything in the brain, he reduces this outside mind to a something which, in his imagination, does the wishing. But what is this wish or thing they call the mind? Of what is it constituted? Where is it located? What are its constituent parts? Answer: Its nature is incognizable; its reality is less than a shadow, and its location is in the mere shady regions of the imagination. Hence, as the physiologist is necessarily ignorant of the nature and powers of this so-called mind, he represents it as something that wishes or wills, for, as in fact it does not exist, this is the best that he can do with his imagination. He knows how the brain and its kindred auxiliaries operate, but he does not know what makes them operate; but if he would read the seventh verse of the second chapter of Genesis, he would see how this wonderful organism was put in action, and know what keeps all its parts in harmonious operation, and would not need to trouble himself concerning this something that the realities of his own teachings so plainly show does not exist. This, however, should not be accepted as derogatory to the study of physiology, for, with the question before you, What is the mind? and with an honest determination to find out, there is but one way that it can be more easily determined. And when we become acquainted with the full reality of things as embraced in the physical organism, not only the fact, but the necessity of the resurrection or re-creation, is plainly manifested in the adaptation of the physical structure to that necessity, and immortality in man is plainly shown to exist only in fancy instead of fact. So that man, stripped of immortality and developed in his true nature, is found to possess nothing that is not mortal except the breath of life. And the fact is plainly developed that those who attempt to unfold the mysteries of the so-called mind are following the delusion of those who teach the immortality of man and his existence independent of the resurrection, and even independent of himself, the absurdity of which is not only plainly and pointedly taught in the Sacred Volume, but is clearly unfolded by the true physiology of man.

Conversion.

In the plan of salvation there are embraced two grand principles or moving causes, the first of which is fear, the other that of love. But these two elements or principles of operation are not, as many suppose, blended in their workings, but, though both may exist and act at the same time, the one is in force or present in that proportion which the other is absent or dormant. And the idea that fear is an essential element in a Christian, is altogether a mistake, for it is only a requisite in the absence of perfect love. Hence, in the work of conversion, love does not woo unless fear has first roused the mind to perceive its danger. For the carnal mind being enmity against God, it cannot be subject to the law of God, which law is love. So, in this case, the man can change his mind, but, though willing that it should be done, he cannot change his heart. For this change of heart is produced not by fear, as the change of mind is, but by the love of God being shed abroad in our hearts, by the Holy Ghost which is given unto us. And hence the difference between Christians and those who are not, for those who are not Christians love as man loves, but Christians love as God loves, because they have the love of God to love with. Hence fear is one element and love another, and, in the practical workings of the plan of salvation, each performs its office. Yet there is not the slightest blending of the two. But as the one performs its duty and retires, so the other supplants it, and operates or rules in its stead. And so fear is an essential in such proportion as love does not exist. Therefore, when love is perfect, so that it controls every action, then fear is fully supplanted by love, and thus perfect love casteth out fear. Hence, notwithstanding that fear is an essential element in the plan of salvation, and is a forerunner of love, it is evident that the proper element to control the Christian is that of love, destitute of all fear; and that he becomes a perfect Christian according as fear recedes and love advances, or in that proportion which love supplants fear. So that when he is a perfect Christian he has that love which casteth out fear. And hence, instead of his being actuated more or less by fear, all his actions are prompted by love, and so he has that faith which does not operate by fear, but worketh by love.

Therefore the work of conversion, though brought about in so many different ways, and seemingly the production of such diverse circumstances, it is, nevertheless, the same one thing, produced by the same cause or causes; and, when fully considered, is found to embrace, first, the fact that man, in his natural state, is not what God requires him to be in order to be and remain His. Or, in other words, he is the offspring of that being who made choice of evil rather than good, and thus brought " sin into the world and death by sin, so that death passed upon all in that all hath sinned." And thus the subject for conversion, or rather of conviction, first understands that he is a sinner; secondly, that as Adam had the privilege to and did choose for himself, so also he has the privilege of choosing for himself, inasmuch as the provision has been made for such a choice. And he realizes that he is guilty and condemned in the sight of God, and that if he remains so that death is the inevitable result; therefore, when the heavenly messenger first shows the sinner his situation, it is terrifying to him; he is afraid of God, he fears to hear His name; yea, the sight of a godly man worries him, and he mentally, if not apparently, trembles at the sight of himself as a condemned sinner. And so it is clearly manifest that fear is the first element or actor in the work of conversion, for the unawakened does not only not have the love of God, but he is destitute of the fear of God. But when the Spirit shows him his true situation, then he sees what he is in the sight of God, and trembles at His name; sees his lost condition, and begins to inquire, what shall I do to be saved? And in this situation fear is all he knows; it moves him, checks him, and surrounds him and gives him no rest until the Holy Spirit, having made him fully sensible of his guilt, his danger, his own helplessness, his utterly lost condition, shows him the provision which has been made for him, exhorts him to comply with its conditions, and accept salvation through the atoning blood and merits of Jesus

Christ; and here it is that he gets the first sight of the love of God. And when he has sincerely repented and obtained forgiveness of his sins through the death and resurrection of God's only begotten Son, then the love of God is shed abroad in his heart by the Holy Ghost; for then the Holy Spirit is given unto him, and is a witness of the loving kindness and tender mercies of God; and then his fears are dispelled and he realizes what the love of God is. And no matter what the capacity of the convert, whether wonderfully great or insignificantly small, this is the reality of the case, no matter how expressed or by whom told. For the conditions of salvation are one, and God is no respecter of persons. His law is one law, and His people are but one. Hence, my unconverted friend, the conditions of salvation admit of no modification, because they are perfect, for God must maintain the dignity of all His attributes. His justice must stand firm; His power and wisdom must be apparent; His mercy must be manifest; His love must be realized; and until you have complied with the terms of the Gospel, and become a partaker of the Divine nature, you cannot belong to Christ. For " if any man have not the spirit of Christ, he is none of His."

But some may inquire, must all this be first understood ? The answer is, no; it must be learned, and if it be asked how much must be known, the answer is, use that which you do know, and learn as fast as you can. If you know that Jesus Christ died for your sins, and rose again for your justification, do not wait to know more; and if you do not exactly understand this, do not wait to find it out; or even if there is something telling you something that you do not understand at all, any further than that it will not allow you to enjoy sin and makes you feel bad about it, do not wait any longer, but go to God in prayer, and the whole thread will be unravelled; and when you have fully understood it, perhaps you will wonder how you found it out. So do not hesitate a moment in endeavoring to secure your eternal welfare, for it is not because you do not know that will keep you out of the bounds of God's mercy, but because you are not willing to know; for God asks nothing of us but ourselves, and this is all that we have to give, and when we do this He gives us all that we need. And it should suffice to secure the confidence of the unconverted to know that God has made them one promise of eternal salvation; yet how many are there, and how easily comprehended as are the following: "Whosoever believeth and is baptized shall be saved." And how simple this belief, for when the eunuch believed with all his heart, he believed that Jesus Christ was the Son of God, and then acted in accordance with his belief. Again, "Repent and be baptized, every one of you, in the name of Jesus Christ, for the remission of sins, and ye shall receive the gift of the Holy Ghost." And again, "That if thou shalt confess with thy mouth the Lord Jesus, and shalt believe in thy heart that God hath raised Him from the dead, thou shalt be saved." And who is it that cannot bring within his comprehension the import of one of these promises and act accordingly? Nevertheless, all that is required is your free will to do so, and God will do the rest. And remember, that the work of conversion is a Divine work; that the first impulse is the prompting of the Holy Spirit, and therefore take courage at the first whisper that calls you to repentance, and be assured that He who has begun a good work in you will finish it to the end. And do not suppose that God needs to be reconciled to you; it is only that you should be reconciled to Him, and therefore God's work in behalf of your salvation is always done, and it only remains for you to do yours, by accepting what He has done. For "He so loved the world that He gave His only begotten Son to die for us, that whosoever believeth on Him should not perish, but have everlasting life." Yet, notwithstanding that God has done so much, that He has done all, and left nothing undone, there are those, and many, who are not willing to trust their case in the hands of Him who died on the cross. They fear to trust Him to mediate their case before the throne of that wonderful benign being who even suffered His only begotten Son to die in their stead. They could do anything else; they could comply with any other requirement of the Gospel, but they could not put their case in the hands of the Lord Jesus and trust their all to Him, who alone is able to save them. And now, my dear, doubting one, in order that you may see yourself as you are, and get rid of your doubts and fears: Suppose yourself to have set out upon an expedition, and in your wanderings to have become entirely lost, and instead of being, as you had been, on an apparently straight road, and in a safe country, you find yourself in a bewildered condition, quite out of the bounds in which you expected to operate; and that when you attempted to regain your former line of travel, your every effort only carried you further into the wilds and dangers from which you were endeavoring to extricate yourself; and continuing your course through this chaotic scene for several days, with everything growing worse, your strength failing you, your companions in the same condition, and unable to render you the least assistance, the sky threatening a tempest, yourself at times immerged in swamp, at others entangled in briars and barely able to continue your journey; and then suppose, just at this epoch of your misery, you find yourself brought to a standstill by the presence of a clift or range, which it is impossible for you to ascend, and yet you fully realize that pass it you must, or there you must perish; and then, while in this deplorable condition, suppose that from out of the gloom that surrounds you, there should appear a gentle form, with pleasing countenance, who, in a sympathetic tone, would earnestly inquire the cause of your calamity, and tell you that though he could not, that there was a certain person that could put you over the barrier, and would be pleased to do so, and that if you would call to him he would give you his assistance immediately; and suppose, also, that this unexpected visitor should tell you that this barrier was the last you would have to surmount, and that as soon as you reached the other side you would be in safety, and have all your wants supplied, that your wounds would be healed, that you would be restored to health and vigor, be surrounded by friends, and that, though at some distance, your home would be in full view; and then suppose that, notwithstanding all this, you turned with disdain from this courteous visitor, instead of gladly following his advice; and then suppose that another, resembling the first, come and tell you the same story, and you answer, "I cannot comply with your counsel; I do not believe that he can raise me over the height, it is so great; moreover, he would not if he could." And then suppose that one of your companions replied, "I will call;" and another said, "I will call;" and so they did call, and as soon as they called, lo, this person did not only answer, but made his appearance immediately, and said, "If you are willing I am ready to place you over, and I assure you that I am able to do so, without doing you the least harm, for I have landed on the other side in perfect safety all who have trusted to my power to do so," and then you say, "Nay, I cannot trust you." And then suppose that one of your companions, who looks more like surviving than yourself, cries out, "Take me and put me over; I will trust you," and the next moment you see him in safety on the heights beyond, and then you hear his deliverer say, "Come, all of you, and be placed safely over, as he is." And you say, "No, I cannot trust you to put me over." My dear, doubting one, do you not see how exceedingly foolish you would be to occupy such a position? And yet this is just the position you occupy. And then suppose that all the rest of your companions follow the example of the first, and are landed safely over, and you hear their mournful groanings turned into songs of rejoicing, and then this mighty succorer turns to you again, and says: "See, they are all safe, and now let me place you with your happy companions," but you reply, "I cannot trust you, you won't save me." My dear, doubting one, this, in reality, is your character; this is the manner in which you treat the offers of Him who alone is able to save you. Yet He does not forsake you. And now suppose that those who had gotten over the barrier call to you and exhort you to place yourself in his arms as they did, and assure you that he can and will do for you just as he did for them, and then endeavor to encourage you by telling you how easily it was done, that they are in safety and that their happy home is in full view, and then beg you to allow him to place you safely among them. And then you say: "Oh, that I were with you; oh, that I were out of this horrible place," and yet you say, "I cannot trust him." Dear, doubting one, accept the sympathy of one who understands your case, but at the same time look at yourself and see how foolish you are. And then suppose that all these friends are at last forced to leave without you, and this wonderful being retires from view, and you are left to pass the stormy night in this, your most deplorable condition, with no prospect of better but everything growing worse; and after passing a night of such wretchedness, without the least appearance of help from any other source, this person, whose best offers and promises you refused the day before, comes even with outstretched arms, and exhorts you to put your trust in him, and re-assures you that he will land you in safety, as he did your companions the day before, and even approaches nearer and in a more earnest tone assures you of his desire to secure your happiness, and tells you that there is no other that can do for you that which to secure your safety must be done, and at the same time you fully realize the fact, but, nevertheless, say: "I wish I could, but I can't trust you." My dear, doubting one, surely you can see how utterly inconsistent your course, under such circumstances must be; yet this is your condition. These are your actions, this is the reality of your case. And can you not, will you not, forego all this inconsistency? Yes, say that you do, and at once fall into the arms of this mighty succorer and be landed safely among your friends, where this your Saviour most gloriously will be the chief.

6*

A Sketch Concerning Doubts After Conversion.

There is a class in the church who are so prone to doubt, and who depend so much upon feeling, that they are scarcely willing to trust that which they see, hear or themselves realize, and at times even doubt their own conversion. But if these would make as good use of their reason as they do of their feelings, yet disregard neither, they would find themselves much less troubled with doubts and more firmly established in the faith. For unless reason rules, feeling may lead astray, and as reason and truth are always in harmony, it would be well for such and all others who are annoyed with doubts, while pursuing a course of conduct which, in the light of the Gospel, recommends itself to their own consciences, to carefully consider that as a man knows that the weather is warm because the sun shines hot, and he is scorched with the heat, so he knows that the weather is cold because the heat is absent and the cold is present; and that this is the way he knows there has been a change in the weather. And he would think one very foolish to tell him there was no change under such opposite circumstances, much less for him to say so himself. Hence this is one way that we may know that we are converted to God. For when we realize that we are at enmity against God, and that we are lovers of and rejoice in doing that which His law condemns, we know that we are sinners just as we know that the day is hot and sultry. But when we realize that these passions or feelings have been removed, and that they have been supplanted by those which are directly opposite as love to God and His children and a peculiar relish for Divine knowledge and holy things, we know that there has been a change just as we know that the day is cool and pleasant, instead of hot and sultry. And this knowledge is a knowledge of conversion, for as such work is the work of the Holy Spirit, the Holy Spirit must be present to do its work.

Communion.

"The Jews, therefore strove among themselves, saying, how can this man give us His flesh to eat? Then Jesus said unto them, Verily, verily, I say unto you, except ye eat the flesh of the Son of Man, and drink His blood, ye have no life in you. Whoso eateth my flesh, and drinketh my blood, hath eternal life; and I will raise him up at the last day. For my flesh is meat indeed, and my blood is drink indeed. He that eateth my flesh, and drinketh my blood, dwelleth in me and I in him."—*John*, VI ch., 52 to 56 v.

Here the question of the Jews was of exactly the same nature as was that of Nicodemus. The Jews said, "How can this man give us His flesh to eat?" Nicodemus said, "How can these things be; can a man enter the second time into his mother's womb, and be born?" Here the two questions are exactly parallel with each other, and the answer of Christ is in exact accordance with the nature of the case, and in the same sense in the one case as it is in the other, so that if He meant that men were to eat His flesh and drink His blood literally, He meant that a man must enter a second time into his mother's womb, that he might be born again. But when Jesus knew that His disciples murmured at it, then

He explained it, saying: "It is the Spirit that quickeneth; the flesh profiteth nothing. The words that I spake unto you, they are Spirit and they are Life." So that inasmuch as it had a spiritual signification, to understand or receive it in a literal sense it would profit them nothing. And as the just are to live by faith, so they are to partake of His humanity through faith, and so live by Him. Hence there was to be a literal method of manifesting this partaking of His body and blood through faith, the conforming to which showed the faith and the necessity of faith in His humanity, as well as in His Divinity, and that His being a man was as necessary for our salvation as His being God was necessary, and that the way was as essential as the life. For it is just as necessary for us to partake of His humanity, through faith, as it is for us to receive His Divinity or Divine spirit, through faith, the difference being that Christ Divinely or spiritually is everywhere present with His saints, and so dwells in them in reality. But Christ, as humanity or man, is at the right hand of God, the Father, and as a man He is man and man only, the difference in Him now and when He was on earth, being that now His body is an immortal instead of a mortal body, and His body having been raised a spiritual body, and having become a glorious body, is just what, and nothing more than, all men will be who are His faithful followers. "For He will change our vile bodies that He may fashion them like unto His glorious body, according to the working wherewith He is able to subdue all things unto Himself."

So this partaking of His humanity through faith is clearly seen from the nature of the case, as well as by the words of His own mouth. And because the language concerning the partaking of His humanity is plain, it does not make the signification any the more literal, but only adds strength to the figure. For, in the first place, the words were plain and positive, and these words that were plain and positive were not flesh and blood in its literal reality, but were spirit and life, and were just as figurative as the rock referred to by the Apostle, for, says he: "They all drank of that spiritual rock, and that rock was Christ," and the literal significance of the one would be as consistent as the other. So that, according to the teachings that Christ meant, they were to eat His flesh and drink His blood, literally, we might as well say that the Apostle meant that they all drank or partook of a literal rock, or that they drank Christ literally, instead of from that rock, which, as a figure, represented Him. And again, it would be just as consistent for them to say, when they eat that which they call the literal flesh and blood of Christ, that it is lion's flesh, or lamb's blood, as it would be to say that it is the literal flesh and blood of a man, for the Scripture calls Him "the Lion of the tribe of Juda," and "the Lamb of God, which taketh away the sins of the world." But, receiving these words as they come from the Lord Jesus, and as He has interpreted them, that they are "Spirit, and that they are Life," we have the fullest assurance of strict compliance with that which these words enjoin, when we receive the bread and wine as a *symbol* of the broken body and shed blood of the Lord. For, at the last supper, (which we celebrate as the Lord's Supper, the celebration of which embraces the form or ordinance through which we partake of His humanity,) "As they were eating, Jesus took bread, and blessed it, and brake it, and gave it to the disciples, and said, 'Take, eat; this is My body.' And He took the cup, and gave thanks, and gave it to them, saying, 'Drink ye all of it; For this is My blood of the New Testament, which is shed for many for the remission of sins.'" And then He tells them that He will not drink of this fruit of the vine which He has just offered them, but at the same time gives them plainly to understand that He will drink it *new* with them in His Father's kingdom. Thus they drank the wine as a symbol of His blood, not that they drank, or thought they drank, blood, for Christ gave it to them for wine, and told them that it was the fruit of the vine, and that He would not drink any then, but would drink it, or the same as that was, in His Father's kingdom. Hence, the disciples no more thought of this being the literal blood of Christ that they were drinking than they thought of Christ drinking His own blood when he got into His Father's kingdom, nor that they were drinking His blood any more than they would be when they would drink with Him of this same fruit of the vine in His Father's kingdom. Moreover, the flesh and blood of the Lord is not God, but man, for God is neither flesh nor blood. So that in partaking of the bread and wine we do not partake of the Divinity of Christ, either literally or figuratively, for it has no reference to His Divinity whatever. The blood of Christ was shed upon the cross, and what was represented by the wine was His blood, for the blood was the life, and when His blood was shed He was dead. But God never died. No; the idea is too absurd to be worthy of notice. So the body or flesh and blood of Christ that constitutes His humanity is all that this ordinance has any reference to whatever, except that it shows the Lord's death till He comes. Thus, when we partake of Christ's humanity it is through this ordinance; but when we partake of His Divinity, it is by receiving the Holy Spirit, which constitutes "Christ in us, the hope of glory." "For if any man hath not the Spirit of Christ he is none of His." For it was not that Christ, as a man, was different from other men, but that He was exactly the same, and in that He is God it is not that He is different from God, but that He is exactly the same. Hence, as Christ taught His disciples that as God He would dwell in them, and that so they should partake of His Divine nature, so He taught them that by or through this ordinance they should partake of His humanity. Thus they partook of the bread and the wine which Christ told them was "His body and shed blood," when as yet His body was not broken or His blood shed, thus placing the fact that it was symbolical of His broken body and shed blood beyond the least shadow of doubt. Hence, by celebrating the Lord's Supper we partake of His humanity in accordance with His testimony concerning it. And the more simplicity there is about a ceremony the more clearly the truth is manifested by it; and all formalities not necessary, or contrary to the original, only tend to obscure it, and hence any deviation from the original form of administering the Lord's Supper can only have a tendency to obscure the great truth embodied in it. For, first these words came from the Lord Jesus Christ; then He defined them, and then, with His own lips, and with His own hands, He performed that ceremony or service that embraced the partaking through faith of His own self. And that which He gave them as a symbol of His broken body was bread, and there is nothing else that will symbolize it; and that which He gave as a symbol of His shed blood was wine, and there is nothing else that can represent it. And, as in this case, so should it be in all others. The Gospel should be adhered to with all simplicity and firmness, and we should ever remember that there is no *something else* that is the Gospel.

Baptism.

"In those days came John the Baptist, preaching in the wilderness of Judea, And saying, repent ye: for the Kingdom of Heaven is at hand. For this is He that was spoken of by the prophet Esaias, saying, the voice of one crying in the wilderness, prepare ye the way of the Lord, make His paths straight. And the same John had his raiment of camel's hair, and a leathern girdle about his loins; and his meat was locusts and wild honey. Then went out to him Jerusalem, and all Judea, and the region round about Jordan, And were baptized of him in Jordan, confessing their sins. But when he saw many of the Pharisees and Sadducees coming to his baptism, he said unto them, O generation of vipers, who hath warned you to flee from the wrath to come? Bring forth therefore fruits meet for repentance."—*Matthew, III ch.*

This was the first voice raised to declare the ordinance of baptism. And that ordinance is just as binding and just as efficacious to-day as it was when John first made it manifest to Israel, and what this ordinance is, no other ordinance can be. And this is the baptism with which Jesus Christ was baptized, that He might "fulfill all righteousness." Thus, if He had not been baptized with this baptism, He would not have fulfilled all righteousness. Notwithstanding that many who came to the baptism of John were called vipers, Jesus showed plainly to the world that none were so righteous as to forego that baptism, by Himself being baptized. Nor did He make His case a specialty, but went out to the river Jordan, where all classes were assembled, and in like manner being baptized. Thus it is clear that Jesus was baptized with the baptism which John preached, and that it was necessary for Him to be thus baptized. Hence, this baptism is *the baptism* without which we cannot fulfill all righteousness; and there is *no other* with which we can. For, though there be other baptisms, without this even Jesus Christ Himself could not have done His part. Therefore, if this baptism with which Christ fulfilled all righteousness, or without which He could not have fulfilled it, is the right one, there is no other that is this same right one. This is the one which John preached and practiced, and it was not administered in a church or a synagogue, neither in the streets of the city, nor in the houses of those who were baptized, but they all went out to the river, and were baptized of him in the river, confessing their sins. Thus is established the fact that John was the first Baptist, that he was in the river when he baptized, and that he baptized in the river; and that the baptism with which he baptized was the baptism with which Jesus was baptized.

And just here are two facts which require especial notice. The first is, "all Jerusalem and all the region round about Jordan," for it must not be supposed that these phrases imply that all the inhabitants of those places went to be baptized, for they are greatly modified by the following, thus: "But when he saw many of the Pharisees and Sadducees come to his baptism," thus showing that it was only many of them and not all, and that the preceding phrases only embraced all those who took the warning to "flee from the wrath to come," who were very many, and constituted a great flocking to John. The other is in regard to the times and length of time that John was baptizing. For John was not only a few days or weeks baptizing or fulfilling his mission, for he did not only baptize, but he first preached the baptism of repentance to the children of Israel; that is, he preached that they should repent and be baptized, believing on Him who was to come after him. And when they had embraced this faith or doctrine, then, as converts to this doctrine, he baptized them. Thus John's baptizing was at such intervals as were proper and necessary, and always in the river. But his preaching was not confined to any particular location because he commenced in the wilderness, for he was manifested to all Israel, even to the chambers of Herod. Thus John had time and opportunity to baptize as many as were converted to his doctrine, and in whatever way his baptism required that it should be done. And this baptism which John preached, and this manner in which John baptized, is the baptism and the manner of baptizing which Jesus accepted, sanctioned, preached and commanded to be preached and practiced, and He never accepted, sanctioned or commanded any other baptism over which man had control. Moreover, this is the baptism in which God, the Father, not only acquiesced, but is that in which He showed His exceeding pleasure by manifesting His own presence at the scene of that wonderful event which neither time nor eternity ever witnessed but once, the baptism of the Son of God. For as soon as he had come up out of the water, lo, the Spirit of God descended, and lighting upon Him, remained. Thus John preached and practiced this baptism, Jesus received and sanctioned it, and God confirmed and sealed it with the visible presence and audible voice of His own self. So that to depart from this ordinance in form is to depart from it in fact, for without the form or formalities, we cannot have the figure; and as the formalities constitute the figure, this figure cannot be constituted by any or of any other formalities, for any other formalities would just as positively constitute some other figure, as these would and do constitute this figure or baptism of John. Hence the difference between baptizing and sprinkling, the one being the truth or the true baptism, and the other simply a mockery; the one proceeding from God and constituting in part the foundation of Christianity, while the other has no existence prior to the partial apostasy, and was a substitute for baptism, which was well calculated to harmonize with the many heathenish doctrines with which the apostates supplanted many of the vital parts of Christianity. And now, as baptism is one of the means by which Christ became perfect, and inasmuch as we are not only permitted but commanded to use the same means, it is evident that we cannot become perfect without it. As the baptism without which we cannot fulfill all righteousness, is the baptism which John preached, that baptism, and that only, is the one which will accomplish the end; and as the form or formalities constitute the figure or baptism, when we conform to or go through the form or formalities which constitute the figure, then we have the baptism; but if the form or formalities be different from this, then it is not this baptism but that *something else* which those formalities constitute. And, as concerning the baptizing by John and baptizing by the Apostles, the only difference between them was that John baptized them on the confession of their sins and faith in Christ as the coming one, and the disciples baptized them with the same baptism on confession of their faith in Christ as the Messiah who had come, as shown in the XIXth chapter of Acts, 1st to 5th verses: "And it came to pass, that while Apollos was at Corinth, Paul having passed through the upper coasts, came to Ephesus; and finding certain disciples, He said unto them, have ye received the Holy Ghost since ye believed? And they said unto him, We have not so much as heard whether there be any Holy Ghost. And he said unto them, unto what then were ye baptized? and they said, unto John's baptism: Then said

Paul, John verily baptized with the baptism of repentance, saying unto the people, that they should believe on Him which should come after him, that is, on Jesus Christ. When they heard this, they were baptized in the name of the Lord Jesus." Thus they were baptized in the name of Jesus Christ, but with the same baptism. In the one case they received the baptism of repentance or were baptized upon the confession of their sins; in the other they had repented of their sins, and were baptized on confession of their faith in the Lord Jesus Christ, to whom the baptism or teaching of John so unerringly directed them. Thus they, as Apollos, were made more thoroughly acquainted with the doctrine of Christ, not that they were in the wrong way, but after they had learned Christ from Paul they were further on in this same one right way or path, which John had made straight, to Christ. For "Apollos was instructed in the way of the Lord and was fervent in spirit, and taught diligently the things of the Lord," without knowing anything more about Him than what John had taught him. Thus the fact that John baptized, that his baptism was the only true baptism; that he was in the river when he baptized; that they went out from the cities and surroundings to him, and that he baptized them in the river, being so clearly shown by the Scriptures that none can innocently deny it, the only question remaining to be settled is, how did he baptize them? which question is answered by the Scriptures, just as definitely as though they had said he placed them under the water and raised them up again. For Paul, in Romans, VI and 4th, tells us that we are "buried with Him by baptism," that is, by being baptized. Thus we see that as John buried the Lord Jesus Christ in the river, so were all these, who in the foregoing were addressed, buried with Him, as He was, in baptism. For there is but one Lord, one faith, one baptism, and this one baptism is that baptism in which the Lord and His followers were buried, the one as or with the other; and thus, being buried with Him in baptism constitutes "the figure whereunto even baptism doth now save us." And Jesus did not only receive and teach the same baptism that John had taught, but, while John was still living, and teaching, and baptizing, Jesus made and His disciples baptized more disciples than John, each at the same time acquiescing in and forwarding the work of the other. Thus it is clearly seen that the baptism of John was the baptism of Jesus, and that as John immersed in the river, so did Jesus or His disciples the same. Again, when on the day of Pentecost the power of God was manifested before that multitude which represented every nation under heaven, and Peter had explained to them the nature of that wonderful manifestation, and had convinced the Jews of their guilt in crucifying the Lord Jesus, and they had been constrained to cry out: "Men and brethren, what shall we do?" Peter said unto them, "Repent and be baptized, every one of you, in the name of the Lord Jesus Christ, for the remission of sins, and ye shall receive the gift of the Holy Ghost." "Then they that gladly received His word were baptized, and the same day were added unto them about three thousand souls." Here we have the peculiar manner of speaking which characterized those times, that is of describing one event as transpiring before another certain event, when in reality it transpired after. For here, according to our mode of speaking, there are described as being baptized about three thousand persons in half a day, yet, when compared with other accounts, and the same mode of description, it will be seen that it is not likely that any of them were baptized upon that day, but the fact that they were added unto them that day is indisputable, for no matter when they were baptized, it was upon that day that they were added unto them, for it was there and then that they believed and received their doctrine. But to make it positive that they were baptized the same day, it would be necessary for it to read thus: Then they that gladly received His word were baptized the same day, and there were added unto them about three thousand souls. And though the Holy Ghost was promised to those who would repent and be baptized in the name of Jesus Christ, it does not follow that they could not be added unto them prior to being baptized, as is plainly shown in the case of Cornelius and those who were with him. For after Peter had entered the house of Cornelius, and had taught them the forgiveness of sins through faith in the atoning blood of Jesus Christ, when he had testified to the fact that God had raised Him from the dead, that himself and others had eaten and drank with Him after He arose from the dead, and that this Jesus who had lived and died and risen again for them was to be the judge of quick and dead, " While Peter yet spake these words," or continued to speak, " the Holy Ghost fell on all of them that heard the Word." Thus Cornelius, and all that were with him, a numerous company, were added to the church in the presence of the inspired Peter, and all that were with him, by being sealed with the Holy Ghost, and manifesting its power and fruit before them, and all this without being or having an opportunity of being baptized, and perhaps without even knowing that they were to be baptized. Thus it is plain that if these could receive the Holy Ghost, and be added to the church, and then be commanded to be baptized, those who received the word upon the day of Pentecost were added to the church upon that day, though they were not baptized until the next or some other day. For Cornelius and his company received the Holy Ghost, spake with tongues, and magnified God, and then, after being added to the church, they were commanded to be baptized. But if Cornelius had asked of Peter the terms of salvation, his answer to him would have been the same as to those upon the day of Pentecost, and the testimony concerning them would have been proportionately similar. Thus, no matter how many, or how few, to be baptized, there is but one baptism. For neither John, Christ nor Peter ever taught or commanded but one; and as in all other cases, so in this of Cornelius, they plainly showed what kind of baptism this was. For after Peter had heard them speak with tongues and magnify God, he said: "Can any man forbid water, that these should be baptized, which have received the Holy Ghost as well as we?" And who could construe such an expression as this to imply that they were to be sprinkled with a few drops of water. For had baptism meant such a process as this, who would suppose that there was not a pitcher of water in such a house as that wherewith he might have sprinkled them all? No, the expression is equivalent to telling them to go to the river, as Christ went, and be baptized as He was baptized. Again, after Paul was converted he was told to "Arise and be baptized and wash away his sins, calling upon the name of the Lord," and whether this washing away of sins is a fact or a figure, it is nevertheless a washing, a complete work that requires much water: and hence Paul says to the Romans, VI and 3d: "Know ye not, that so many of us as were baptized into Jesus Christ, were baptized into His death? Therefore we are buried with Him by baptism into death: that like as Christ was risen up from the dead by the glory of the Father, even so we also should walk in newness of life. For if we have been planted together in the likeness of His death, we shall be also in the likeness of His resurrection." Thus we see that if we have been baptized at all, we have been baptized into His death with that baptism wherewith we have been buried, for we have been baptized into His death by being buried with Him; not with Him in the grave, but with Him in baptism. Hence it is as plain and as easy to be understood that those who are baptized with the baptism which Christ was baptized with, are immersed —buried under the surface of the water—as it is to understand that a friend was put under the surface of the ground when we are told that he was buried with his oldest brother. Therefore, how audacious the act of coming into the presence of God with such a mockery as sprinkling, and teaching it as the reality of baptism. Not once does the thought seem to have been entertained by the writers of the Scriptures, or those to whom they were written, of construing baptism, or the manner of baptizing, to be anything other than immersion; nor does there occur within the lids of the New Testament a single sentence to justify the act of sprinkling as even a substitute for baptism, under any circumstances whatever, much less to make it baptism. Again, when Philip had expounded the Scriptures to the Ethiopian eunuch (whose case the Lord had made a special one), and had preached unto him Jesus, "As they went on the way, they came unto a certain water: and the eunuch said, See, here is water; what doeth hinder me to be baptized?" Thus we see, that while preaching to him Jesus, Philip preached to him baptism, or else he would not have desired to be baptized. "And Philip said, 'If thou believest with all thine heart thou mayest.' And he answered and said, 'I believe that Jesus Christ is the Son of God.' And he commanded the chariot to stand still; and they went down both into the water, both Philip and the eunuch; and he baptized him. And when they came up out of the water, the Spirit of the Lord caught away Philip, that the eunuch saw him no more: and he went on his way rejoicing." Hence, this case is the same as that of Cornelius, for if Philip had wanted to sprinkle the eunuch, the eunuch would have commanded his servant to bring a vessel of water for that purpose. And considering the dignity of the eunuch, and the ease with which the ceremony could have been performed, it is doubtful as to whether either would have got out of the chariot. And it is evident that if Philip had taught the eunuch that sprinkling was baptism, he would have thought him beside himself to have asked him to wade into the river in order to have a few drops of water sprinkled upon him. But such was not the case. The place was adapted to the necessity, as Philip had previously taught the eunuch. Hence, when the eunuch saw the river or body of water, he knew that in it he could be buried, and that that would constitute the baptism which Philip had taught him. So this inspired Philip, and this previously dark-minded heathen, without ever thinking of such a thing as sprinkling, went down into the water, both of them, and Philip baptized him, and, thus buried with Christ in baptism, he came up out of the water, and went on his way rejoicing; and how any one acquainted with

Scripture can go on his way rejoicing in a way so contrary to this, is mysterious indeed, and cannot debar the conclusion that sprinkling is apostasy, and that instead of its being a part of Christianity, it is only a mockery of the same.

The Soul.*

The fact that there is a close connection between the soul and the spirit is so obvious, from everything connected with the case, that it is not even to be supposed that it would be disputed. For the Word teaches that this union is as close as the joints and marrow, or the thoughts and intents of the heart. Yet it teaches that the soul and spirit are two, and as different as the joint is different from the marrow, or that the thought of the heart is different from the intent, and needs but the plain language of Scripture to make its certainty unquestionable. For, says the Apostle: "The Word of God is quick and powerful, and sharper than any two-edged sword, piercing even to the dividing asunder of soul and spirit, and of the joints and marrow, and is a discerner of the thoughts and intents of the heart." Thus, notwithstanding that men call soul spirit, and spirit soul, and say that both are one, the Word of God divides them asunder and shows that they are two, and tells us the difference between them. And inasmuch as the term soul occurs so frequently, and, as might be said

---

* NOTE.—While perusing this, the reader should carefully attend to that which his Bible teaches, instead of that which he has learned from the pulpit or any particular creed.

under such peculiar circumstances, or in connection with such circumstances as to render its significance very difficult, the first fact that should be understood, and which should be kept constantly in view in determining its meaning as made use of in the various parts of Scripture, is, that no matter how it is used, or to what being, class, or part of a class it may be applied, that being or class of beings to which the term soul is applied must constitute that which the term soul or souls represents, even if that is God's own self. And, with this fact in view, it will be easily seen that the difficulty in determining the meaning of the term soul in all its applications, exists in the erroneous teachings of man concerning the nature of and the future state of man, instead of any Scriptural mystery whatever. For the soul is not a distinct entity from the being man in any respect whatever, for the being man is embraced in the term soul. For the body, the physical organism, was the man; then this man, through the operation of God's breathing into his nostrils the breath of life, became a living soul; then this man was not what he was before, an inanimate being. But this heretofore inanimate being became and was a living soul; so that a soul is what he was; not that a soul was put in him, but, the breath of life being put into him, a soul is what he became; so certainly a living soul is what he was, it could not be that he was anything else. And as the nature of things in the present life and that which is to come, as taught in the Holy Scriptures, is so vastly different from most of the teachings of modern times, so it will be seen that the nature of death is also vastly different. For, notwithstanding that death is a result of sin, God will not allow it to be ultimately triumphant; neither has He allowed it to triumph, except as especially confined to the man. "For God is not the God of the dead, but the living; for all live unto Him." He is the God of Abraham, the God of Isaac, and the God of Jacob, yet He "is not the God of the dead, but of the living; for all live unto Him." When God pronounced upon man the sentence that he should die, He also determined in connection with that sentence, or had determined prior to his existence, that his death or being dead should be but for a time. And when man dies, he is dead so far as relates to himself and to all around him, and, thus dead, the sentence is executed. But with respect to his being dead to his Creator, that seems to bear an impossibility upon its face, for, in the first place, God made man, and made him of a particular material which Himself had made; and, when man was made of that particular material, then God breathed into that man's nostrils the breath of life, and he became a living soul. Then, when the breath of life was separated from him, he was dead, but the breath of life was the same, and the material of which he was made was the same; so the breath of life was with God, and the dust was the same dust; and the workmanship that was dissolved was God's own work. So that, notwithstanding the sentence of death was executed upon man,

man was not dead to his Creator. "For the hour is coming in the which all that are in their graves shall hear the voice of the Son of God, and come forth." That is, all that are dead shall hear His voice and come forth. Hence man, upon whom the sentence of death was executed, who is dead unto himself and dead to all around him, unknown to himself, devoid of all animation, can hear the voice of Him to whom the Eternal has consigned his destiny, and hear it so distinctly that he will come forth. Hence, how plain, how very plain, is this fact that man is not dead to his Creator; for, if it were so that a father could call to his son, or a son to a father, that was laid in the grave, and he was to come forth alive, it would be folly to call him dead—if death represented the same idea that it does now. Therefore, it is evident that man lives unto his Creator, for he will hear the voice of the Son of God and come forth, not from that celestial clime that exists in the imagination of those whose ideas better fit them to teach the history of the gods and goddesses than the realities of the Scriptures, but from the grave, for it is those who are in their graves that are to hear His voice and come forth. Hence, God is not the God of the dead, but of the living, for all live unto Him. Again, as regards the creation of man, the breath of life is that which God breathed into his nostrils, and through this was brought about his animation, or through or by it he became an animate instead of an inanimate being. So that the difference between man and soul is, that the man is the being that was made of the dust of the ground, and the soul is the being which the man became when God breathed into his nostrils the breath of life. Hence, man is the *organism inanimate*, and soul is the same *organism animate*. Hence, it is that wherever, whenever, or in whatever connection it may appear, that soul means the living man and all that man is, whether in this world or that which is to come, or wherever it may be. And now, that inasmuch as to accumulate all the times, ways and subjects that are connected with the term soul, or to which it relates, would be altogether unnecessary and more calculated to weary than instruct, to select from all these a sufficient number of examples to show its use and manner of use in the different ages of the world, together with the most difficult ones, or those which would be considered the most difficult, it seems would be the most agreeable and instructive. Thus, the first use that was made of the term was to declare that when God breathed into man's nostrils the breath of life, that *man* became a living *soul*. Then, when in Exodus, chapter XXX, 11th, 12th and 13th verses, it is made use of, it shows that soul means self. Thus: " And the Lord spake unto Moses, saying, When thou takest the sum of the children of Israel after their number, then shall they give every man a ransom for his soul unto the Lord, when thou numberest them; that there be no plague among them, when thou numberest them." That is, that each should give a ransom for himself that was numbered, so that, being ransomed, there would be no plague among these souls that were numbered. A half-shekel was what they were to give. The rich should not give more, and the poor should not give less, than half a shekel, when they gave an offering unto the Lord to make an atonement for their souls. That is, for themselves, for each was under the necessity of making an offering for himself. Again, in Leviticus, XXVIth chapter, 15th verse: "And if ye shall despise My statutes, or if your souls abhor My judgments, so that you will not do My all commandments, but that ye break My covenant; I also will do this unto you;" and so on. In this, the threat is against them if they shall despise His statutes, or if their souls abhor His judgments; in the 43d verse it is "because they despised My judgments, their soul abhorred My statutes." So that *ye* and *they* are represented as doing, and *soul* is represented as doing the same thing, so that in the repetition there is no discrimination between *ye*, *they* and *soul*. For, if they despised His statutes, and soul abhorred His judgments, who was it that was to be punished? And if they despised His judgments, and their souls abhorred His statutes, who is it that was punished? For *soul* did what *they* did, and *they* did the same things that *soul* did. The question is easily answered, for it teaches nothing other than that the soul means self. I Samuel, XVIIIth chapter, 1st verse: "And it came to pass, when he had made an end of speaking unto Saul, that the soul of Jonathan was knit with the soul of David, and Jonathan loved him as his own soul." That is, Jonathan's affections were centered upon David, and he loved him as he loved his own self. The matter rested between Jonathan's own self and David's own self, and it was that one loved the other. And it must be remembered that as man became a living soul, and a soul is what he is, that phraseology must in its sense bend to the fact, and not the fact bend to the phraseology. Job, XVIth chapter, 4th verse: "I also could speak as ye do: if your soul were in my soul's stead, I could heap up words against you, and shake mine head at you." That is, if it were yourself instead of myself, or if you were in my place or situated as I am, I could do as you are doing. XIXth Psalm, 7th verse: "The law of the Lord is perfect, converting the soul: the testimony of the Lord is sure, making wise the simple." Here the simple that were made wise are part of those souls who were converted. And the Lord said unto Peter: "When thou art converted, strengthen the brethren." So that *thou*, Peter's self, was converted, and *soul* is represented as being converted; so that when Jesus addressed Peter, if He had said: When thy soul is converted, strengthen the brethren, He would surely have meant when thou thyself art converted. XXII Psalm, 29th verse: "None can keep alive his own soul." That is, none can keep alive his own self, or none can keep himself alive. And how foreign to common sense it would be to say that none could keep alive his own soul, if the case with it were as is taught in modern times, that a soul cannot die. XXVth Psalm, 13th verse: "His soul shall dwell at ease, and his seed shall inherit the earth." That is, himself shall dwell at ease. "His seed shall inherit the earth." That is, the seed of that soul that dwells at ease, shall inherit the earth. How plain it is that *soul* and *self* are identical. XXXIVth Psalm, 2d verse: "My soul shall make her boast in the Lord: the humble shall live thereof, and be glad." That is, himself would make his boast in the Lord, and when the humble or righteous heard that a soul of such dignity as David boasted in the Lord, they would be glad. XLIXth Psalm, 15th verse: "But God will redeem my soul from the power of the grave: for He shall receive me." That is, He would bring him forth at the resurrection, and then receive him; and thus David would be satisfied, having awakened with his likeness. CVIIth Psalm, 9th verse: "For He satisfieth the longing soul, and filleth the hungry soul with goodness." The longing soul is the person who longs, and the hungry soul is the person who is in want, and who is the recipient of God's goodness; and what folly to deny that *soul* means *self*, when such facts as these are presented before us. Xth Prov., 3d verse: "The Lord will not suffer the soul of the righteous to perish, but He casteth away the substance of the wicked." He will not suffer the righteous soul to famish: but if the righteous were treated as the wicked, then these righteous persons or souls would famish for want of that substance which was cast away. XIIIth Prov., 25th verse:

"The righteous eateth to the satisfying of his soul: but the belly of the wicked shall want." That is, the righteous eateth to the satisfying of Himself, or to the satisfying of his appetite, but the wicked were not to have the wherewith to satisfy their appetites. Jeremiah, XXXIst chapter, 12th to 14th verses: "Therefore they shall come and sing in the height of Zion, and shall flow together to the goodness of the Lord, for wheat, and for wine, and for oil, and for the young of the flock, and of the herd, and their soul shall be as a watered garden; and they shall not sorrow any more at all. Then shall the virgin rejoice in the dance, both young men and old together: for I will turn their mourning into joy, and will comfort them, and make them rejoice from their sorrow. And I will satiate the *souls* of the priests with fatness, and My people shall be satisfied with My goodness, saith the Lord." Their souls should be as a watered garden: that is, they themselves should be refreshed and invigorated, so that they should sorrow no more; for their condition would be so changed that the virgin would rejoice and dance in company with the young and old together, for their mourning was to be turned into joy, and they were to be made to rejoice from their sorrows. That is, they themselves, those souls, were to rejoice. "I will satiate the souls of the priests with fatness." That is, He would bestow more upon them, or place more in their hands than they could make use of, so that this people could not fail to be satisfied with His goodness; thus it was the priests themselves that were satisfied, as confirmed by XXIst chapter and 25th verse: "For I have satisfied the weary soul, and I have replenished every sorrowful soul." How plainly is it to be seen that these writers knew that man became a living soul, and that a soul was what he was, and that they knew nothing of any other kind of a soul. Ezekiel, XIVth chapter, from 12th to 16th verses: "The word of the Lord came again to me, saying: Son of man, when the land sinneth against Me by trespassing grievously, then will I stretch out Mine hand upon it, and will break the staff of the bread thereof, and will send famine upon it, and will cut off man and beast from it. Though these three men, Noah, Daniel and Job, were in it, they shall deliver but their own souls by their righteousness, saith the Lord God. If I cause noisome beasts to pass through the land, and they spoil it, so that it be desolate, that no man may pass through because of the beasts: Though these three men were in it, as I live, saith the Lord God, they shall deliver neither sons nor daughters; they only shall be delivered, but the land shall be desolate." Here God declares that if Noah, Daniel and Job were in the land that "they should deliver but their own *souls* by their righteousness." And again, He says that *they* only should be delivered, thus showing plainly that their own souls meant their own selves, for it was *they* only that should be delivered. Ezekiel, XVIIIth chapter, from 1st to 20th verses: "And the word of the Lord came unto me again, saying, What mean ye, that ye use this proverb concerning the land of Israel, saying: The fathers have eaten the sour grapes, and the children's teeth are set on edge? As I live, saith the Lord God, ye shall not have occasion any more to use this proverb in Israel. Behold all souls are mine; as the soul of the father, so also the soul of the son is mine: the soul that sinneth, it shall die." (Quite different from being immortal.) And so, then, souls that are His are the souls who, if they sin, shall die. "But if a man be just, and do that which is lawful and right (that is if one of these souls be just), and hath not eaten upon the mountains, neither hath lifted up his eyes to the idols of Israel, neither hath defiled his neighbor's wife, neither hath come near a menstruous woman, And hath not oppressed any, but hath restored to the debtor his pledge, hath spoiled none by violence, hath given his bread to the hungry, and hath covered the naked with a garment; He that hath not given forth upon usury, neither hath taken any increase, that hath withdrawn his hand from iniquity, hath executed true judgment between man and man, Hath walked in my statutes, and hath kept my judgments, to deal truly; he is just, he shall surely live, saith the Lord God. (Yes, this person is a soul that shall not die). If he begat a son that is a robber, a shedder of blood, and that doeth the like to any one of these things, And that doeth not any of these duties, but even hath eaten upon the mountains, and defiled his neighbor's wife, Hath oppressed the poor and needy, hath spoiled by violence, hath not restored the pledge, and hath lifted up his eyes to idols, hath committed abomination, Hath given forth upon usury, and hath taken increase; shall he then live? he shall not live; he hath done all these abominations; He shall surely die; his blood shall be upon him. (Yes, all souls are the Lord's, and the soul that acteth thus shall surely die.) Now, lo, if he begat a son, that seeth all his father's sins which he hath done, and considered, and doeth not such like, That hath not eaten upon the mountains, neither hath lifted up his eyes to the idols of the house of Israel, hath not defiled his neighbor's wife, Neither hath oppressed any, hath not withholden the pledge, neither hath spoiled by violence, but hath given his bread to the hungry, and hath covered the naked with a garment, That hath taken off his hand from the poor, that hath not received usury nor increase, hath executed my judgments, hath walked in my statutes, he shall not die for the iniquity of his father, he shall surely live. As for his father, because he cruelly oppressed, spoiled his brother by violence, and did that which is not good among his people, lo, even he shall die for his iniquity. Yet, ye say, why doth not the son bear the iniquity of the father? When the son hath done that which is lawful and right, and hath kept all my statutes, and hath done them, he shall surely live. The *soul* that sinneth it *shall die*, the son shall not bear the iniquity of the father, neither shall the father bear the iniquity of the son: the righteousness of the righteous shall be upon him, and the wickedness of the wicked shall be upon him." Here the soul is pictured as being all that the man is, whether good or bad, and all souls are the Lord's, and all this people is represented under the head of souls. The soul that doeth righteousness, he shall surely live, and the soul that sinneth, he shall surely die. Here is the fact in its plain form, and the phraseology is such as cannot be mistaken, showing in the most comprehensive manner that soul means self, that the man's self is the soul, or that a living man is a soul, and that there is nothing more or less that is or even can be a soul; so that it is impossible for a soul to exist without embracing all that man is, for these were souls and nothing more; and, hence, to be souls hereafter they can be nothing less. Matthew XVIth chapter, 26th verse: "For what is a man profited, if he shall gain the whole world, and lose his own soul? or what shall a man give in exchange for his soul?" Lose his soul, lose his self; for who is it that is lost, or what is it that is lost? All is lost that is not saved, and there is nothing saved when the soul is lost, so all is lost, and that all is himself. Romans, XIIIth chapter, 1st verse: "Let every soul be subject unto the higher powers." This is the fact presented more in accordance with modern phraseology, and shows in the plainest possible manner that every soul meant every man. I Peter, IIId chapter, 20th verse: "Few, that is, eight souls, were saved by water." Who is it that does not know who these eight souls were, and who could know who they were without knowing that soul meant self? These souls were Noah and his family; and Noah being a soul, and his wife being a soul, and all his family being souls, it would be strange indeed if all their offspring were not souls, and then it would be wonderfully strange if these souls were not their own selves. For it was Noah's own self that built the ark, and it was this soul, Noah, and the other seven souls that were saved in it. I Peter, IVth chapter, 19th verse: "Wherefore, let them that suffer according to the will of God, commit the keeping of their souls to Him in well doing as unto a faithful Creator." That is, commit the keeping of their selves to Him, for it was in their doing that they were to commit their selves to Him. II Peter, IId chapter, 14th verse: "Having eyes full of adultery, and that cannot cease from sin, beguiling unstable souls." If it could be made to appear that these souls did not belong to humanity, then it would be one step towards disproving that soul meant the living being, man, or rather that which the man became. But, contrarywise, it is so plain as to need no comment, but itself speaketh and tells us that soul means self. The revelation of John, the Divine. What is the revelation of John, the Divine? There is no such a thing as the revelation of John, the Divine; the phrase is a hoax. There is "the revelation of Jesus Christ which God gave unto Him to show unto His servants things which must shortly come to pass, and He sent and signified it by His angel unto His servant, John." So that, in the first place, it is the "revelation of

Jesus Christ." Secondly, it is that which "God gave unto Him," for the purpose of showing unto His servants things which must shortly come to pass, and He sent and signified, or made it known, by His angel unto His servant, John, "who bare record of the word of God and of the testimony of Jesus Christ, and of all things that he saw." That is, he bare record that it is the revelation which God gave unto Jesus Christ. Then he bare record to the fact that he has the testimony of Jesus Christ, to the effect that it is the revelation that God gave unto Him; and then he bare record to all that he saw. So that the difference between John and us, in respect to these things, is that they were pictured before his vision, and he wrote them for us to read. And when we read them we know just as much about them as he did, the difference being that he saw the picture and we have the picture described by him. He heard the words, and he tells us what he heard. In the first place, he tells us that he was in the "isle that is called Patmos, for the word of God, and for the testimony of Jesus Christ." That he "was in the spirit on the Lord's day, and heard behind him a great voice as of a trumpet, saying, I am Alpha and Omega, the first and the last, and what thou seest, write in a book, and send it unto the seven churches that are in Asia." This part of the revelation was concerning things that were, and is distinct from the rest of the revelation, being confined to the things that then were, and was received before that he was invited up to heaven. But it must not be supposed that there is any such an idea presented as that John was in heaven, but he says, "I was in the spirit on the Lord's day." Not his own spirit, but the spirit of the Lord, and it was through the power of that spirit that his vision was carried to heaven, that he might see and understand these things, that he might communicate them to us, not as one who had heard or read of them, but that he might tell us that which he had seen and fully realized was and was to be. Thus God has not only told us of these things, but John, being of our brethren, He has showed them unto us. Yet John did not see any reality of things whatever. There was nothing that passed before his vision that was reality; it was only a picture of that which was thereafter to be realized, and he did not see any reality of souls under the altar, any more than he saw the sun become black as sackcloth of hair, and the moon become as blood, which did not come to pass for more than seventeen hundred years after. Nor did he see them any more than he saw the heavens depart as a scroll when it is rolled together, or that the great day of God's wrath had come. All that was pictured before him was that which was to be thereafter. There was no present reality about it whatever. So that when he says he saw under the altar the souls of them that were slain for the word of God and for the testimony which they held, the case with them was the same as with the rest that he saw. So that when he says that he saw these souls under the altar he means that he saw them just as he saw the sun become black as sackcloth of hair and the moon become as blood, which he never saw at all. So that this that is shown under the fifth seal is a figure pointing to the reality of things, as represented in the XXth chapter, when he saw the souls of them (or those souls as it is evident that the original was) that were beheaded for the witness of Jesus and for the word of God, and which had not worshiped the beast, neither his his image, neither had received his mark upon their foreheads or in their hands, which souls lived and reigned a thousand years. That is, first he saw these souls, then he saw who they were, that they were those persons who had been beheaded, and then were resurrected, and then he saw that they lived and reigned with Christ a thousand years. Then he says that he saw that the rest of the dead lived not again until the thousand years were finished. So that the souls that he saw then were the resurrected righteous that were not of that number which did not live, but were still dead, so that the resurrected righteous are here represented by the term soul. And before a soul can exist in a future state, that soul must first be resurrected, for it is the animate and not the inanimate being that is the soul. And these persons whom John saw were the identical beings who were slain for the word of God and for the testimony which they held. That is, those souls that died, those souls that were resurrected, they are the souls that lived and reigned with Christ a thousand years. So that, except with respect to its glorification, whatever a soul is here that is exactly what it will be hereafter, for there is no soul except the being which the man became, and this being was nothing more or less than a soul. Hence, to be a soul, it is necessary to be all that living humanity constitutes.

The Spirit of Man.

When God breathed into man's nostrils the breath of life, he became a living soul. But though a perfect man before God breathed into his nostrils the breath of life, he did not live. So that without the breath of life, he was an inanimate being; but after the breath of life had been breathed into him, then he was an animate or living being. Hence, when he was deprived of this breath of life, he again became an inanimate being. And the Word says that the body without the spirit is dead, so that of course the body with the spirit is alive, just as was the case with the damsel, for her spirit came again, and she lived; so that this inanimate damsel was made to live by causing her spirit to come again. And Adam was made or became an animate being by receiving the breath of life. Now, the damsel that had lived, but was dead, was restored to life by giving her back her spirit; and if Adam, who had been deprived of the breath of life, had had that breath of life restored to him, then he would have lived, just as he did at the first, and just as the damsel did. So that as they were both inanimate, the one destitute of the breath of life, and the other destitute of her spirit, and the receiving of the breath of life caused the animation of one, and the receiving of her spirit caused the animation of the other, the fact that the spirit of man is the breath of life is positively manifested. But it must not be supposed that the breath of life is simply the atmosphere, otherwise a pair of bellows might live; but it is that cause of animation, that something without which we cannot exist, that something which returns to God who gave it: that is the breath of life or the spirit. So that, as the spirit returns to God, who gave it, and the breath of life is all that we know of as regards the creation of man that God gave unto him, it is evident that whatever the breath of life is, that is the spirit. And the word spirit, no matter when or how used, must have a distinct literal or a distinct figurative meaning, and the phraseology connected with the term must conform to the primitive fact, and not the original fact to the many modes in which it is used; and therefore, as the spirit of man is a reality, the term in its literal sense only is applicable to it. And as the breath of life is the spirit, that spirit, it seems, must be the spirit of life; and the spirit of life from God entered into the two witnesses, and they stood upon their feet, or lived, just as the damsel did when her spirit came again. So that it is evident that the breath of life, the spirit, and the spirit of life from God, are identical; and thus the difference between man and soul exists in the presence or absence of the spirit: in the *absence* of the *spirit*, it is the inanimate man; when the *spirit* is *present*, it is the living soul. So then, inasmuch as man is of the dust of the ground, and the soul is that which the man became when God breathed into him the breath of life, and inasmuch as the breath of life, the spirit of life from God, and her spirit, are one and the same, the question is, what is the breath of life? And the first thing to be remembered is, that it is not only the breath, but the breath of life, that animating quality that was adapted to the organic structure, man, and was that which God breathed into him; that which did not constitute his existence, but that made animate the being that did exist. Hence, what folly to suppose that the spirit of man is a distinct entity, with all the personal appearance, the peculiar characteristics, and, in fact, all that the man is, except what they call the prison-house of this imaginary being which they call the spirit. To believe this because there are beings that are and were created spirits, comes no nearer the standard of common sense than to suppose that these beings which are and never were anything else but spirits, possess the peculiar ability to become, and will become, human beings. But, foregoing all this absurdity, we see that the man is the being, and that the spirit is the breath of life; and that when this being, man, received the breath of life, he became a living soul; and that when the breath of life is taken away, that that breath of life is what and all that the spirit is. It is not the *man*, nor the *soul*, but the *animating power* by which THE ONE BECOMES THE OTHER. Yet, still the question to be determined is, what is the breath of life? And, in so doing, it is necessary for all to discriminate between the spirit of man and the spirit of God, and also between the spirit of God and the spirit of life from God, and again between the term spirit in its literal sense and when used figuratively. For the terms, a haughty spirit, a contrite spirit, are figurative, and represent that which the same characters or persons are noted for, and at the same time embraces both character and person of the beings thus represented, and in reality signifies a haughty person or a contrite person, with no particular reference to spirit whatever. And the phrase "Be ye renewed in the spirit of your minds," shows to what extent this figure may be carried. Hence, it must be remembered that in determining what the spirit of man is, the literal significance of the term is all that is applicable to the case, as are the following: Ecclesiastes, XIIth chapter, 7th verse: "Then shall the dust return to the earth as it was: and the spirit shall return unto God, who gave it." This presents the case in its simple reality, and shows that the organic structure dissolves and returns to the earth as it was, and that the spirit, the breath of life, returns to God, who gave it; and that, in consequence thereof, the soul is not in existence, for the soul was the being that the man became by receiving the breath of life, and, hence, when this departed and the organic structure which it animated returned to its dust, and the dust to the earth as it was, the soul could not be in existence until resurrected or re-created, when, having received the breath of life or the eternal life, it would again be that living soul which it was before. But the Psalmist, VIth, 5th verse, continues this inspired strain, and plainly shows that the preceding and following were all that they knew about the nature of death. For says he: "In death there is no remembrance of Thee: in the grave who shall give Thee thanks?" That is, what man? Who can remember Thee in the grave? Who can give Thee thanks from thence? For my dust will be as other dust, and my spirit will have returned to God who gave it, and until I awake in the morning of the resurrection I shall be no more. And in the CXLVIth chapter and 4th verse, still he continues: "His breath goeth forth; he returneth to his earth; in that very day his thoughts perish." All this points with unerring precision to the fact that when the spirit returns to God who gave it, that the being, the soul, ceases to exist, and that they are not, and that "till the heavens be no more they shall not awake nor be raised out of their sleep." And it is thus that the righteous rest from their labors, for there is no reward until the resurrection, as shown in the VIth chapter of Revelation. For these did rest, and it was said unto them that they should rest a little longer until the appointed time, as revealed in the XXth chapter. For it is the being which the man became, the soul, the self, that is to exist and be rewarded or punished, and not the breath of life. And as the first existence of man was brought about or wrought by the Almighty, so the second or re-existence will be the result of the mighty power of God, by the same or a similar operation. And, therefore, when He calls forth the man from the dust and endows him with life, then he will have again become a living soul. And now the question is, is the breath of life the one and the same breath of life, as that of which the man was made was the one and the same one dust? Now if, when God created Adam, He had made ten men, He would have breathed into the nostrils of the first the breath of life, and then He would have breathed into the nostrils of the second the same breath of life, and then He would have breathed into the others the same breath of life which He had breathed into the first two, so that they would have all received the one and the same breath of life which God breathed into Adam. Hence, it follows, that when the breath of life of these ten men returned to God, it would be the same one breath of life. Therefore, as the breath of life, the spirit, and the spirit of life from God, are all one and the same, the spirit of all men must be that one and the same spirit or breath of life; thus, this spirit, or spirit of life, or breath of life, is the spirit or breath of life of us all, just as that of which we are made is one and the same one dust. So that all are made of the same one dust, and the same one breath of life is the breath of life of us all.

The Judgment and the Judge.

"And I saw the dead, small and great, stand before God, and the books were opened." And what books were opened? were they the Old and New Testaments, or the books in which the deeds of mankind were recorded? The theory or notion that is so nearly or quite universal, that the books that were opened were those in which the deeds of mankind were recorded, when properly analyzed is found to be quite foreign to the reality of the case. For though, as was said, another book was opened, which was the book of life, the dead were judged out of those things which were written in the books aside from the book of life, according to their works. Not according to their works as written in the books, but out of the things which were written in the books, according to their works. Hence, there were at least three books; that is, first the books were opened, which is positively more than one but seems to imply but two. And as the Bible is positively two books, and in reality but two, and as the word that Jesus spake was to judge them at the last day, and he also in whom the Jews trusted, even Moses, was to judge or accuse them, it is evident that the books that were opened were not the records of actions, but the Old and New

Testaments. And after this judgment, all those whose names were not written in the book of life were cast into the lake of fire. But this book is the Book of Life of the Lamb slain from the foundation of the world, and therefore it must not be supposed that they were written in it from the foundation of the world, but written in the Book of Life of the Lamb slain from the foundation of the world. Thus it is that at the judgment the Word of God that now is and has been preached to the world, is that word which is to judge it, or by which it is to be judged at the last day.

In determining the question of judgment it is necessary to have a clear understanding of those parts of Scripture which bear directly upon the final scene, in order that not only the nature of the judgment may be understood, but that the nature, character and person of the judge may also be fully comprehended. For a knowledge of things as existing before Christ is a prerequisite to a proper understanding of the nature and character of the judge and the reality of the judgment. And inasmuch as it hath suited the fancies of so many to endorse and promulgate the idea that the Ancient of Days became the son of a woman, it is necessary to understand the reality of the prophetic writing from which this delusion had its origin. For, though they say, cannot God do all things, are not all things possible unto Him, it does not follow that because God is omnipotent that we are to believe all the disgusting absurdity that monks, and priests, and college-bred sophists see fit to teach, even if there were no Scriptures to prove the contrary, much less when God's Word presents the truth in all holy harmony, and perfectly consistent with Divine wisdom, and makes it so plain that the half wise can understand it if they will. In the seventh chapter of Daniel, commencing at the ninth verse, we read: "I beheld till the thrones were cast down, and the Ancient of Days did sit, whose garment was white as snow, and the hair of his head like pure wool: His throne was like the fiery flame, and his wheels as burning fire. A fiery stream issued and came forth from before him: thousand thousands ministered unto him, and ten thousand times ten thousand stood before Him; the judgment was set, and the books were opened. I beheld then, because of the voice of the great words which the horn spake, I beheld even till the beast was slain, and his body destroyed, and given to the burning flame. As concerning the rest of the beasts, they had their dominion taken away: yet their lives were prolonged for a season and time. I saw in the night vision, and, behold, one like the Son of man came with the clouds of heaven, and came to the Ancient of Days, and they brought Him near before Him. And there was given Him dominion, and glory, and a kingdom, that all people, nations and languages should serve Him: His dominion is an everlasting dominion, which shall not pass away, and His kingdom that which shall not be destroyed." Here the prophet presents before us, in the most comprehensible manner, the reality of that which transpired after the resurrection and ascension of Jesus Christ. For it was a scene that was to transpire not upon earth, but in heaven. Hence, in the nineteenth chapter of Luke, eleventh and twelfth verses, we read: "And as they heard these things, He added and spake a parable, because He was nigh to Jerusalem, and because they thought that the kingdom of God should immediately appear. He said, therefore, a certain nobleman went into a far country to receive for himself a kingdom, and to return. And he called his ten servants, and delivered unto them ten pounds, and said unto them, occupy till I come." Here Christ in reality told them that He was not to receive His kingdom then, but that a long journey intervened between that time and place, and the time and place of His receiving it. And when He entered upon the reality of that parable and took His journey, He went to receive for Himself a kingdom and to return. And it was then that He, the one like the Son of man, or the Son of man, was seen by the host of heaven coming with the clouds that received Him out of the sight of the apostles at His ascension. And after His arrival in the heaven of heavens He was brought before the Ancient of Days, for here it was that He received from the Ancient of Days dominion and glory and a kingdom that all people, nations and languages should serve Him, And from this, the time of His receiving this dominion and glory and kingdom, He is waiting or expiating till His enemies be made His footstool, when He will come again in like manner as He went into heaven. *For He was to receive for Himself a kingdom and then return.* Yea, just as the host of heaven saw Him arrive there, so will the inhabitants of the earth behold Him when He shall return, except that as when He went He went to receive honor and glory and power; when he returns to the earth He will have and display the glorious realities of that honor and glory and power that He received from the Ancient of Days, when He was brought before Him. And here is presented the two persons as plainly as language can picture them, the one like the Son of man, the other the Ancient of Days; the one who was enthroned in the heaven, the other the one who was brought before Him; the one He who received dominion and glory and a kingdom, and the other the one who bestowed these gifts; the one the Father, the other the Son, a reality of two as much as Abraham and Isaac were two. And why was it that Daniel saw and described one like the Son of man, or one resembling the sons of men, coming with the clouds of heaven? Why is this such a notable fact that one like the Son of man came with the clouds of heaven, and was even brought before the Ancient of Days? Surely, if the theories of the present day were correct, it would be nothing strange, or worth a prophet's telling about, for hundreds and thousands resembling the sons of men to arrive in heaven. But the reason is obvious; such an event never transpired before; one resembling the sons of men never arrived there before. He was a stranger in heaven, for that was the far country to which He was to go, and the scene before the throne embraced the significance and displayed the reality not only of that which then transpired, but also of the wonderful events connected with His presence there. The first was the fact that far from that celestial region had transpired an event with which the scene before the throne was in perfect harmony, as a result of that event. And hence there was seen, not a God, that was the son of a goddess (of course there is none), but one resembling the sons of men, coming with the clouds of heaven. Now, if the mother of Jesus had been a goddess, Jesus would not have been man at all, there would not have been the least spark of humanity in Him; and just the same in regard to His Father, for Mary being His mother, if Joseph had been His father, there would not have been the least spark of Divinity in Him. But as Mary was His mother, He was man, and not God only; and as He was begotten of God instead of being begotten of Joseph, He is God, and not man only, just as He is man and not God only. So that, just as He is man because He was born of the Virgin Mary, so He is God just because He was begotten of God. And God never assigned any other reason for His being His Son, and Jesus never claimed to be the Son of God or to be Divine for any other reason. Here we see that this being was the Son of man, not a resident of heaven, but that in His journey from His native distant clime in the cloudy chariot. He had just arrived there and was conducted into the presence of the Eternal, and was no more that Eternal or Ancient of Days than Isaac was Abraham, but was just the being that God declared Him to be when He said: "Thou art My Son, this day have I begotten thee," and just what Christ claimed to be, the Son of God, because the Ancient of Days, or Jehovah, was His Father. Hence we see that the one who is ordained to be the judge of quick and dead is the Son of Mary, the Son of man, the Son of the Ancient of Days, or Jehovah. And we see that this judge is to be the monarch of creation, for all are to serve Him, whether peoples, nations or tongues; there will not be even one, not even a tongue, that will not praise Him. Again, we see that He is not unacquainted with the nature of man and the realities of his case, for He is God and man, and thus omniscience combined with human sympathy. He is qualified to decide for God and man. His omniscience God understands exactly, and is satisfied for Him to be the judge, or else He would not have made Him such. And we are assured of His sympathy with man in that He is even now our great High Priest, that can be touched with the feeling of our infirmities, and so He is qualified to be an impartial judge. And this is He whom the heavens hath received until the time of the restitution of all things, for when He ascended on high the heavens received Him and must retain Him until that day which God has appointed in the which He will judge the world in righteousness, by this His

Son, whom He hath ordained to be the Judge; and hence the declaration, "Behold He cometh with clouds," (just as He went,) and every eye shall see Him, and they that pierced Him, and all nations shall mourn because of Him (that is, the wicked of them). For He hath received of the Ancient of Days dominion, and glory, and a kingdom, the establishing of which is to embrace the sweeping away of all that is unholy, all that is unfitted to dwell in His kingdom. No wonder that the nations are to mourn when they behold this august personage coming in the clouds of heaven to establish His kingdom. For all transgressors are to be rooted out of it, the wicked are to be destroyed from off the face of the earth. Yea, "the heavens, being on fire, shall be dissolved, and the elements shall melt with fervent heat; the earth, also, and the works that are therein shall be burned up." No wonder, then, that in the minds of the wicked there is a fearful looking for of judgment and fiery indignation that will devour all His adversaries. For, having completed His work as mediator, "the Lord will descend from heaven with a shout, with the voice of the Archangel, and with the trump of God. And the dead in Christ shall be raised," and together with His living followers the doors will be shut about them till His wrath be passed, till the wicked shall be consumed from off the face of the earth, till the heavens be dissolved and the earth shall have passed through its fiery ordeal, and is brought forth in all its Eden loveliness and fitted for their everlasting abode, "then shall the righteous shine forth in the kingdom of their Father." Then will be established the dominion; then will be realized the glory in that kingdom, which the one like the Son of man received from the Ancient of Days, when they brought Him near before Him. Before Herod the Great received his kingdom, he went to a far country, even to Rome, and appeared or was conducted before Cæsar, and received the kingdom or dominion of Judah, and was made its king there before the universal monarch, then returned to Jerusalem, destroyed his enemies and reigned over his territory or kingdom, and displayed that power which he had received in the far country, when he was brought or conducted before the Cæsar and senate of Rome. And Jesus Christ left Jerusalem as literally as Herod did, and went to heaven as literally as Herod went to Rome, and appeared before the Ancient of Days as literally as Herod appeared before Cæsar, and received of the Ancient of Days dominion and glory and a kingdom as literally as Herod received dominion and a kingdom from the Roman power, and will return to the earth, destroy His enemies and take possession, as really as Herod returned from Rome and took possession.

The Devil, or Satan and Hell.

It is evident that in the notions of the world and the teachings of most ecclesiastics concerning the devil and hell, there are as great mistakes as there are in regard to many other subjects or characters that do not come within the bounds of our visual comprehension, and when the true nature of the case as revealed in the Scriptures is understood, it is plain to be seen that these errors concerning the character and operations of Satan, and the nature of hell, are productions of the great heresy concerning the future state. For as the church, after the apostasy, had a heaven for all its saints to enter at death, where they were ushered into the full reality of eternal felicity, so they prepared for the wicked a burning hell, where at death they were punished with everlasting torments. And thus, by this heretical process they frustrateth plans of the Almighty, and transformed the resurrection and judgment into what might in reality be called the scum of a farce. And this hell, or place of everlasting burning, they created a sort of kingdom for Satan, over which he had supreme control, and those called devils were his subordinates; and so they represent Satan in hell executing the decrees of the Almighty as his willing and obedient servant. And that here in this burning hell, Satan and all the devils are continually delighting themselves in burning their victims and witnessing their agony, which is nothing more than executing and acquiescing in the pleasure of the Almighty. No wonder that the Apostle saw that damnable heresies were to be brought into the church. This is substantially the teachings of the Papal church concerning hell and the devil, and is just what the outside world understand concerning it, and is also the teachings of most the Protestant churches. This might do for the heathen, from whence it was derived, but, alas, what ideas for Christians to entertain. For they are as directly opposite to the teachings of Scripture as falsehood can be to fact. Hence, when we forego all these absurdities and accept the truth as revealed in the Scriptures, we see that the only hell of punishment is the lake of fire that was prepared for the devil and his angels, and that though the wicked are to be cast into it after the last resurrection and the judgment, the devil has no more to do with the punishing of the wicked than they have to do with punishing him. And that instead of the devil being the superintendent and chief of hell, and the punisher of the wicked, that he never was in hell, and that he is just as much afraid of it as a murderer would be; yea, and much more, and has better reasons for being afraid of it. For he was a murderer from the beginning, and abode not in the truth, and for rebellion against God he was cast out of heaven into the earth, which has ever since been the field of his operations. Hence we read that he tempted Christ in the wilderness, not in hell, and Christ said that he (the devil) was the one who sowed the tares among the wheat, but not in hell. Again, we read that he is the one that sets snares for the unwary of mankind, and the Scriptures tell us that he goeth about as a roaring lion, seeking whom he may devour. He also contended with Michael, the Archangel, about the body of Moses, but not in hell. The devil was to cast some of Christ's followers into prison, but not in hell. All these are the operations of the devil, and all are confined to this earth, while his presence in that fiery kingdom over which he is represented as reigning is not once brought to view. He is represented as being busily engaged on the earth, which received him when he was cast out of heaven. But such a thing as his being in hell even for an hour is not so much as intimated. Hence we see that the operations of the devil are always intermingling with the affairs of mankind, and confined to this earth, where " he goeth about like a roaring lion seeking whom he may devour." But this devouring is quite different from what is generally imagined, for it is manifest that he does not, nor does not want to, devour every one he comes in contact with, or else he would not need to go about seeking. Yet " he goeth about as a roaring lion, seeking whom he may devour." Hence it is evident that he is not seeking those who are already his own, but those who are not. But while he goes about as a roaring lion, he does not go roaring as a lion roareth; but as a lion, when he goeth about seeking for something to devour, uses all his energies in the most stealthy manner possible, so the devil does not roar as a lion, but as the lion hastens unobserved to the scene of action, and uses all his powers to conceal his presence and deceive his victim until it is within his grasp, so the devil uses the craft of the roaring lion, conceals himself, and deceives his victim until it is within his power. And while the lion has the various hiding-places that the forest afford him, from which he bounds upon his prey, so the devil has much better concealment, and many more hiding-places from whence he attacks to destroy the sheep, and especially the lambs of Christ's flock, which flock alone is his prey. For he is the prince and power of the air, that spirit which now works in the hearts of the children of disobedience. And he goeth about as a roaring lion goeth about when he is seeking that which he may devour; not with roarings, but with all the stealth and deceit that by his workings he can put into the hearts of the children of disobedience. And thus enthroned as the prince and power of the air, with his operations confined to the earth, he will continue to be such until shut up in the bottomless pit for a thousand years. And when he is released for a little season his operations will again be confined to earth, until, not as the king or ruler of perdition, but as a subject for hell, he will be cast into the lake of fire, which, according to the teachings of Scripture, will be the first hell, he ever was in, and the first time he ever was in it.

The Finale of the Earth, the Righteous and the Wicked.

"Seeing then that all these things shall be dissolved, what manner of persons ought ye to be in all holy conversation and godliness."—*II Peter, III ch.*, 11*th v.* The being dissolved, the death or dissolution of the earth, and its resurrection, change or being made new, is not only in perfect harmony with the nature of things as a recovery from the curse and its effects, and its being fitted for the eternal abode of God's ransomed people; but it is as clearly shown in the Scriptures as the life, death and resurrection of man. Hence, as when man had fallen and incurred the displeasure of the Almighty, and the sentence of death was pronounced upon him, so was the curse pronounced upon the ground for his sake. Thorns and thistles it was to bring forth to him, yea, it was to be his sepulcher, it was to be a land of thorns and thistles, instead of everything that was good, wholesome and pleasant. It was to produce for him only in the sweat of his face. Toil and sorrow was all that it presented to his view; it was cursed for his sake. And who is it that cannot see that there is something wrong upon the face of the earth? Who cannot see, amid all the sorrows and miseries of this life, that the present state of things is not the work of an all-wise God, that it is not consistent with Divine wisdom to place man amid such a state of things as now exists, to toil through years of sorrow, to enjoy nothing except in part, and that only at the expense of twice or thrice its value in sorrowful toil, with the assurance before him that he is born to sorrow as the sparks fly upwards, and every circumstance that happens around him, all that he sees, hears, or is capable of comprehending, teaching him that the earth is cursed? Yea, everything teaches us that it is not consistency to suppose that an all-wise God created man to live and toil, and toil to live, and live out his days in sorrow, just for the purpose of living a life that on such a basis would not be worth living for. No, it is charging God foolishly; it is altogether contrary to His wisdom. Hence it is evident that the present state of things did not always exist, and that they are not to be continued or be allowed to continue indefinitely. And it seems that men ought to be capable of comprehending the reality of the earth's being cursed, for whatever cause or by whatever power, even if there were no Scriptures to tell them that it was so. Yet, laying all this aside, and following the teachings of the Sacred Volume, we see that the earth is cursed, and that its dissolution is decreed. And as man was to die and return to his dust, so the earth was to die or be dissolved and return to its original state, without form and void; and as the man was dead to himself and to all around him, and still lived unto his Creator, so the earth was to be dead to man and its present condition, yet not unto God. For as man, when resurrected or re-created, will be the same being, so when the earth is brought forth in all its Eden splendor, though new or made new, it will be the same earth, just as the man will be the same man. For as the workmanship which constituted the man was dissolved, so the workmanship of the earth is to be dissolved. Yet new things are not to be created, but old things are to be made new. For when He says, "Behold I make all things new," He does not say that He makes all new things. No, it is the old things which are to be made new. And what folly for anyone to admit that God created the earth and man, and then to contend against the idea of a resurrection or re-creation; for, surely, if the creation of the earth and man is possible, its being re-created or made new is quite as possible, and much more probable, having the one fact to sustain the other. Hence, as regards the creation of the earth, its being cursed, its life or duration, its death or destruction, its resurrection or being made new, we have these facts as plainly taught and as pointedly presented as those embracing the past, the present and the future state of man. Thus, in the beginning God created the earth and the heavens in beauty and perfection, and the earth and everything that moved upon it reflected, as it were, the smile of God's countenance, for they were His workmanship, and God acquiesced in His work by declaring that everything which He had created was good. Thus God smiled upon all creation and all creation smiled. But when man, unmindful of his solemn obligation to his Creator, who had endowed him with the dignifying attribute through which his obedience was to be the result of his own will, and the choice of life or the choice of death was to be his own choice; when man, unmindful of the position that he occupied, unmindful of that dignifying attribute that he possessed, which placed him second only to Divinity, stooped from his lofty and dignified position, and deigned and dared to accept the forbidden fruit from the hand of woman, and thus preferred her favor to that of his Creator, in order to punish him for his disobedience, the ground was cursed for his sake. Its beauties were transformed, its luxuries were tainted, the ever brilliant heavens were beclouded, and storm and tempest, scorching heat and chilling winds, disease, anxiety and never-ceasing toil, pain, misery and death at once supplanted all that glorious precedence of this sad event. And thus it has continued for nearly six thousand years, without the least mitigation, or the least indication in the powers of nature that points to a recovery from that condition to which, through the disobedience of man, the earth was necessarily subjected. Thus proving that nature is not God, but that God is the God of nature, and that He can place her in chains and set her free at His pleasure. That "He speaks and it is done," and that nature only echoes the fact that she is servile, that she is not God, but that God is Jehovah. And as it is evident that the earth has lived out nearly all its days, and that the destruction by fire of the present state of things, as presented in II Peter, IIId chapter, 10th verse, is God's own way of returning them to that which they were before the fall of man, and before the earth was infected with the curse which made its dissolution and return to its original condition necessary to its purification and cleansing from the curse and its effects, and its being renewed and fitted for the everlasting abode of his ransomed people; this being God's own method, it is evident that when, as shown in the 13th verse, the earth is brought forth, though new, it will be the same earth, for its renewing will make it new, and its re-creation will constitute its being created. For the meek are to inherit the earth, and Abraham was promised the ground upon which he stood, "and the kingdom and the greatness of the kingdom under the whole heaven is to be given to the people of the saints of the Most High God, and they shall reign on the earth." And the kingdom of Christ is to be a kingdom to which there is to be no end. And the kingdoms of this world are to become the kingdom of our God and of His Christ. Hence the kingdoms or dominions of this world are to constitute the kingdom of Christ, notwithstanding that this world, as it now exists, is to be destroyed. For He is to reign from the river to the ends of the earth, and the earth renewed is to be that earth to the ends of which He is to reign. And the greatness of the kingdom under the whole heaven, is to be the greatness of His kingdom. He is to be king of kings and lord of lords; that is, He is to be king of kings as Nebuchadnezzar, Alexander and Julius Cæsar were kings of kings; and He is to reign in the New Jerusalem, which is to be the capital of His kingdom in the new earth or the earth renewed, as literally as Nebuchadnezzar reigned in Babylon, or Julius Cæsar reigned in Rome. And His personal presence will be just as much a reality in the New Jerusalem, as it was when He stood before Pilate. Thus the finale of all the thread-work of the Scriptures, as regards the earth and its destiny, is consummated with the glorious realities of the kingdom of Christ and Christ its king, who is to reign over His ransomed people from the river to the ends of the earth. And thus the meek are to inherit the earth, and delight themselves in the abundance of peace. And that which God promised to Abraham before his death, that will he realize in the new earth or the earth renewed, after his resurrection, and so will all the righteous realize. For the glorious realities of the Kingdom of Christ are just the reality of their hope. And terrible as it is (and terrible enough it is), that which is pictured in the XXth of Revelations, is to be the finale of the wicked, "For yet a little while and the wicked shall not be." "The wicked shall be destroyed from off the face of the earth." "The transgressors shall be ruled out of it." The lake of fire is their destiny. "They shall consume, into smoke shall they consume away." They are to be destroyed; they are to be no more forever. For as the literal presence of the organic structure, in the case of the saint, constitutes his existence, so the absence of the organic structure, in the case of the sinner, constitutes his non-existence. As the saint is consigned to eternal life, so the sinner is consigned to everlasting death, the one being that which the other is not. So that as the *eternal life* of the saint *constitutes his reward*, so the *everlasting death* of the sinner *constitutes his punishment.* For as death is destroyed there can be no more death, and the saint is beyond its bounds forever. And as the resurrection is past and the wicked are destroyed thereafter, there is no more life forever, and so they are consigned to an everlasting death, which is their everlasting punishment.

How it was that Moses was Present at the Transfiguration.

"And after six days, Jesus taketh Peter, James, and John his brother, and bringeth them up into a high mountain apart, And was transfigured before them: and His face did shine as the sun, and His raiment was white as the light. And behold, there appeared unto them Moses and Elias talking with Him."—*Matthew, XVII.*

Here in the transfiguration we have a type of that reality—His coming and kingdom, or His presence in His kingdom—and here also is a representative of the living righteous, in the person of Elias, and a representative of the dead in the person Moses. But the question is, how came Moses there? If man can be nowhere present except personal, how is it that Moses, who had died and was buried, could have been present with Christ and His companions on the mount, for he was there and talked with Jesus? This is forcing the truth fairly, for Moses was there as really as was Peter, James or John. But again, the question is, how came he there, for he had died and was buried? This is easily accounted for, and only needs the plain language of Scripture and a little reason to remove all doubts, and make his personal presence there as easily to be understood as though an angel had been there. For the Word says that "Michael the Archangel, when contending with the devil, he disputed about the body of Moses, durst not bring against him a railing accusation, but said, the Lord rebuke thee." Now, what did they want to dispute about the body of Moses for? Where was the body of Moses? Just prior to this event the body of Moses was just where it was buried, or otherwise it had returned to its dust; and thus the case stood just prior to this event. But the most likely of the two is that it was just after his burial that this transpired. But let the case be as it may, the body of Moses was what was in dispute, but the devil could do nothing until Moses was or was to be resurrected; neither was there any cause for action on his part, for so long as death reigned he was satisfied, but when there was a prospect of a resurrection to life, then he comes forward to contend against it. And because there are to be two resurrections in the future, it does not follow that there has not been special resurrections in the past. For not only was Christ and many of the saints raised, but Jesus gives us plainly to understand that there were resurrections prior to that time. For, saith He, "As the Father raiseth the dead so the son quickeneth whom He will." Thus we see that the Father had already raised the dead, and why not Moses one of them? Verily he was, or else he would not, he could not, have taken part at the transfiguration, for the whole affair was a personal affair. There was no spirit there. There were Peter, James and John, and these three were the companions of Jesus, whom He took with Him to be witnesses of that which was there to transpire. And it was the man Jesus, the Son of God, the Son of Mary, who took them there, and was there and was transfigured before them. But when He was transfigured He was not transmuted, for the difference between Him then and before consisted in the development of His Divine nature in that halo of glory that the Apostle endeavors to describe, and when this passed His appearance was the same as before. Thus it was the person Jesus before He was transfigured, the same person while transfigured, and the same person afterwards, and the person whom they looked upon while on the cross was the same person that they looked upon while on the Holy Mount, whose appearance they describe as so glorious. Therefore it was the person Jesus who was there, and Elias was there, and of course personal, and his presence there was to establish the truth as presented in I Corinthians, XV, 51. And Moses was there to establish the fact that though a man die, yet shall he live again. For this man Moses had died and was buried, and his being dead, or his continuing in death, seems to have been something to which Satan paid particular attention. For, in the first place, Moses was dead, and as long as he remained so Satan could do nothing; there was nothing for him to do. But God having made his case a special one, and determined that he should be resurrected, dispatched Michael, the Archangel, to take possession of the body of Moses. And Satan, who had not feared to contend against God, did not fear to contend with this mighty messenger in order to prevent the resurrection of the man Moses. This is the only reason that can be given for the contention about his body, which resulted in the defeat of Satan and the resurrection of Moses. And therefore, the reason why Moses was at the transfiguration was because he had been resurrected. He was there as literally as he was in Egypt; he was there with Christ and His companions as really as He was with the Children of Israel, and if he had not been resurrected he could not have been there, for it was Moses and Elias who talked with Jesus, or else it was not Jesus who talked with them. It was Peter, James and John, Christ, Moses and Elias who were there.

Who Preached to the Spirits in Prison?

" For Christ also hath once suffered for sins, the just for the unjust, that he might bring us to God, being put to death in the flesh, but quickened by the spirit: By which also He went and preached to the spirits in prison; Which sometime were disobedient, when once the long suffering of God waited in the days of Noah, while the ark was a preparing, wherein few, that is, eight souls, were saved by water."—*I Peter, III ch.*, 18*th*, 19*th and* 20*th vs.*

" Put to death in the flesh." So then He was dead and destitute of spirit, but He was " quickened by the spirit: By which also He went and preached unto the spirits in prison," that is by the spirit by which God went, not Christ, for Christ was put to death, and then He was quickened by this same spirit by which God went in the days of Noah, and preached to those who were alive at that time.

When did He go? In the days of Noah. And how did He go? Why, by His spirit. And this embraces *God personally and God spiritually*, and such in the days of Noah. So that it did not mean Jesus, but Jehovah, Whose spirit the Holy Ghost is. Hence, as He went there spiritually, and preached to them, so He went to the sepulcher, where His Son Jesus lay dead, and quickened Him, for Jesus was dead, and the spirit which or by which God preached to the antediluvians hundreds of years before that time, went to the sepulcher of Jesus and quickened Him. So that it was not Jesus who went and preached by the spirit, or went by the spirit, but Jehovah, His Father, who had done it hundreds of years before Jesus was begotten by the Holy Ghost. Hence, as this is the positive reality of the case, the only difficulty, if any, is in the phraseology, that is, in the manner in which these two facts come to us. Yet, when the passage is properly analyzed and reason allowed to operate, all difficulty is easily removed. "For Christ once suffered for sins." This is one fact. "The just for the unjust." This is another fact. "That He might bring us to God." This is another fact. "*Being* put to death in the *flesh.*" This is another fact. "But quickened by the *spirit.*" And this is another fact. Hence we see that *He* is understood before *being*, in put to death, and that *of God* is understood after spirit, in quickened by the spirit. And, therefore, we see that the original or positive reality of the passage is that Christ, also, hath once suffered for sins, the just for the unjust, that He might bring us to God, *He* being put to death in the flesh but quickened by the *spirit of God*. By which also He, *God*, to whom Christ brought us, went and preached to the spirits in prison. So that if we accept the facts in our own phraseology, its simplicity becomes one of its prominent features, and thus we read it: For Jesus Christ once suffered for sins; He, being just or perfectly innocent, suffered for or instead of the unjust or guilty, that He might secure our release from the condemnation which our guilt incurred, by His thus atoning for it, and so bring us to God, for He was put to death and so died in our stead; but upon the third day after His crucifixion God, His Father, quickened Him by His spirit. And then we would take up the other circumstance and describe it, or rather we would have taken it up before, inasmuch as it transpired thousands of years before the above. And perhaps we would say that in the days before the flood Noah spake and warned the people, as he was instructed by the Holy Ghost, the same as the prophets did in after times. And then we would have in our own mode of speaking the reality of the twentieth verse. Again, if we compare this, the 18th, 19th and 20th verses of I Peter, III chapter, with that of Hebrews, V chapter, 6th and 7th verses, we see that the above solution is positively confirmed by both phraseology and fact. Sixth verse: "As He saith also in another place, Thou art a priest forever after the order of Melchisedec." Seventh verse: "Who in the days of his flesh, when he had offered up prayers and supplications with strong crying and tears unto Him who was able to save from death, and was heard in that he feared; Though he were a son, yet learned he obedience by the thing which he suffered." Here, in the 7th verse, *Who* positively relates to Melchisedec, whereas taking the fact in the case, *Who* positively relates to Christ. So that if we lay aside the fact and accept the phraseology, it was Melchisedec who did what the reality of the passage shows that Christ did. Therefore this is precisely the same in construction as the 18th and 19th verses of III chapter of I Peter, except that it is by *which* in one and *who* in the other. So that in Hebrews Christ is meant, instead of Melchisedec, and in Peter, Jehovah is meant instead of His Son Jesus. And therefore we see that it was Jesus, the Son of God, who was dead, and that this same being was quickened by the same spirit by which God, His Father, preached to the antediluvians in the days of Noah. And whether the reality in the abstract, or as embraced in the present constructions, determined it, it was Jehovah, and not Jesus, who went by the spirit. For *God* is understood after spirit, in the 18th verse of I Peter, III chapter, and thus dispenses with *by also* and *He* in the 19th verse. So that, according to both phraseology and fact, it was not Jesus, but Jehovah, who went and preached to the spirits who were then in prison. And, therefore, to present the fact in our own phraseology, the simple and positive reality is, that after Christ had been put to death, God, His Father, quickened Him by His spirit, and that this spirit is the same spirit by which He inspired Noah, who proclaimed the Divine word to those around him, while, as God had commanded him, he was building the ark for his own safety. And, therefore, the answer is, that it was Jehovah, the Father of Jesus Christ, who went and preached to the spirits in prison many hundreds of years before Jesus was begotten.

The Spirits in Prison.

"For Christ also hath once suffered for sins, the just for the unjust, that He might bring us to God, being put to death in the flesh, but quickened by the spirit: By which also He went and preached unto the spirits in prison."—*I Peter, III ch.*, 18*th and* 19*th vs.* Thus Christ died, "the just for the unjust, that he might bring us to God," *He* "being put to death in the flesh but quickened by the spirit," *of God*, which, in the days of Noah, dictated to him that which he preached to those around him while the ark was a preparing. Therefore these spirits in prison are the persons who were disobedient in the days of Noah, and to whom the Gospel had been preached, so that the preaching of the Gospel is the preaching of God's truth, and no matter where or when preached, whether by the Prophets or by Jesus Christ, it is the dictates of the same spirit, and is the same one truth or Gospel. And thus all to whom the Word of God has been preached, whether dead prior to the preaching of the Gospel of Jesus Christ or not, are to be judged by the same truth as men living then, for all having the same word of truth preached unto them, whether living or dead at that time, all are to be judged according to that one truth or Gospel that had been preached unto them.

Thus, the Gospel having been preached to those who were dead, who had lived in the days of Noah, it is plain to be seen that these spirits in prison are those persons who had lived in the days of Noah but who, at the time of Peter's writing, were dead, and who were referred to in the 6th verse of the IVth chapter: "For, for this cause was the Gospel preached also to them that are dead, that they might be judged according to men in the flesh, but live according to God in the spirit." "Be judged according to men in the flesh," that is, as though they were then living. "But live according to God in the spirit," that is, the Word was preached to them that they might have eternal life the same as those to whom the Word was preached at that time. And having eternal life they would come forth at the resurrection as those would who were then living, and so live according to God in the spirit, which spirit would be their life, that is, if they had believed. And now the question is, how are these persons spirits, and what is the prison? The term spirit is so vague in its meaning, and covers so much ground, that its signification can only be determined by the manner in which it is used, and the surroundings of the subject to which it is applied, and, of course is figurative or literal in its meaning. And as it is impossible for the dead to have the Gospel preached unto them, the term spirit, as applied to those who were in prison, must be figurative and represents those persons who lived in the days of Noah, and then had the Gospel preached unto them, who were then dead and in their graves, which were their prison, and were spirits according to the phrases: These troublesome spirits, he is such a perverse spirit, he is a different spirit altogether. So that the spirits in prison, those dead ones who had lived in the days of Noah, and were such perverse spirits that even in the presence of the building of the ark, they rejected the Word of God to their own destruction, and thus became the dead who had had the Gospel preached unto them, and who at the time of Peter's writing were captives or prisoners, for though Christ had led captivity captive, the general releasing had not taken place, and these still remained in their graves, the prisoners of death, as plainly shown in the IId chapter of Job, where he says, " Why died I not from the womb? Why did I not give up the ghost when I came out of the belly? Why did the knees prevent me, or why the breasts that I should suck? For now I should have lain still and been quiet, I should have slept: then had I been at rest, With kings and counsellors of the earth, which built desolate places for themselves; Or with princes that had gold, who filled their houses with silver. Or as a hidden untimely birth I had not been; as infants which never saw light. There the wicked cease from troubling and the weary be at rest. There the *prisoners* rest together; they hear not the voice of the oppressor. The small and the great are there; and the servant is free from his master." And so all who in the days of Noah had the Gospel preached unto them are there, for the *prisoners rest together*, the great and the small are there. Here we see that the little innocents, the kings, the counsellors and princes, that had gold, who filled their houses with silver, all rest together. They are the great and the small who in the grave, their prison, are the captives of death, for " there the *prisoners* rest together."

Christ's Answer to the Thief.

"And he said unto Jesus, Lord, remember me when thou comest into Thy kingdom. And Jesus said unto him, Verily I say unto thee, to-day shalt thou be with me in paradise.—*Luke, XXIII ch., 42d and 43d vs.*

There is a great deal of phraseology in the Scriptures that seems to baffle the wisdom of the present day, but the facts of Scripture, though so grossly perverted, when traced to or from their primitive sources, are simple and harmonious. But it is nothing strange concerning the phraseology, when we consider the different hands through which they have passed; and the fact that the Papacy had ruled supremely so long before the Reformation; and the fact that the erroneous idea that at death all passed to heaven and received their reward, or went to perdition and were punished, had become the most prominent feature in the teachings of the Papal church. When these things are taken into consideration, it is not strange to suppose that the monster heresy concerning the future state had much to do with the phraseology of the Scriptures, and particularly of the New Testament, as it is now among us, and especially with respect to this subject, and in regard to this particular text it is evident that its present construction was generated by or through the predominance of the great error concerning the future state. But if the text had been translated thus: Because thou has spoken thus, I say unto thee, that thou shalt be with me in paradise; or had it been: I say unto thee this day, that thou shalt be with me in paradise—which would be in perfect harmony with the phraseology of those days—then the construction would be in harmony with all the facts that encircle the subject. But as it is, it is in accordance with the erroneous idea concerning the future state, which, during the supremacy of Papacy, did, and now does, absorb the thoughts of most teachers of Scripture, to the exclusion of everything that conflicts with it; and so they have added error to error, until many of the vital truths of Christianity are placed in obscurity, and these flying fancies not only flaunt but reign supremely. And through this mite of the translators' phraseology, they would sacrifice those vital truths without which the whole compact would be a farce. But, placing the comma after *day*, instead of after *thee*, and the sentence constructed thus: Verily I say unto thee this day, that thou shalt be with me in paradise, it is in perfect harmony with all other Scripture. But the construction that makes it appear that upon that day the thief was with Him in paradise, is contrary to all truth. It makes false Christ's words to Mary, and is also at variance with His words to His disciples, when He said: "Handle Me, and see; for a spirit hath not flesh and bones, as ye see Me have." And this person who addressed them was the same person who addressed the thief, and who had lain in the grave till the third day, who after He had risen from the dead told Mary that He had not yet ascended. Thus He made them to understand plainly that He was the same persen then that He was before, and that His mission upon earth was not yet finished. And the fact that He had lain in the grave from the time of His crucifixion until His resurrection was so positively implied and so clearly understood that it is hardly common sense to suppose that it would have been expressed. And it should be remembered that the writers of those days wrote without periods. colons, commas, or any other points or stops. And hence it is evident that the inserting of the comma after *thee*, and the present construction of the sentence, is in accordance with the erroneous idea that has been mentioned. And inasmuch as the original had no such pause to denote such a meaning, it is far more consistent to place the comma after *day*. Moreover, as this thing of pointing did not belong to the original, there can be no importance attached to the inserting of the comma after *thee*, instead of after *day*, except that it was the notion of the translators concerning its meaning that induced it. So take out the comma and let all judge for themselves, for every one has as good a right to determine its meaning, in accordance with the language and sense, as the translators had. For it is the infallible Word of God that we are to depend upon and reverence, and not the fallible notions of its translators. Again, with respect to the present construction, it is not in harmony with the request of the thief, or the nature of the case and its surroundings, but is altogether the contrary, and is in direct harmony with the heathen notion concerning the future state. For the request of the thief embraced the one simple fact, that is, that Christ would remember him when He came into His kingdom, just as Job implied that God would remember him in accordance with his request, that He would hide him in the grave, that He would give him a set time, and remember him. For at that time neither the thief nor anyone else had any idea of a kingdom this side of the resurrection, and hence, the object of the thief was to obtain through the promise of Christ the hope of Israel, the resurrection from the dead. And knowing that they were both to die, the thief realized that there was no hope this side of the resurrection, and he, looking beyond the resting in the grave, called upon Jesus to remember him when He came into His kingdom. Hence it is evident that in the answer of Jesus there was no such an idea conveyed as the present construction indicates. And how unreasonable to suppose that Christ would teach His disciples to look to the resurrection, and the establishing of His kingdom, and instruct them to teach the same, and then tell a thief that upon that day he should be with Him in paradise; and how inconsistent to cling to such an idea, when everything teaches the contrary, with nothing but the winged fancy of the translators to establish it. Again, this part of the history of that great event seems to be that which was told the writers by others, and notwithstanding that John was present and that Jesus conversed with him while hanging on the cross, it is evident that the conversation between the thief and Jesus, if such took place, escaped his notice, and it is evident that the writers upon this subject recorded this conversation as told them, and not as they had heard or received it from any Divine authority. For John, who it seems would be the best authority, has nothing to say about it, and Matthew "says that the thieves that were crucified with Him cast the same in His teeth," that is, they derided Him the same as did the Jews; not one of them, but both. And Mark, after describing the manner in which they mocked Him, says, " and they that were crucified with Him reviled Him." Thus the testimony of these two broadly contrasts with that of the third, for Luke, who it seems would be the least authority for such a record, tells us that one of these thieves was quite a different being from the other, and treated the Lord Jesus in quite a different manner from the other, inasmuch that, in the most penitent manner, he asked the Lord to remember him when He came into His kingdom, and that the Lord's answer was, "Verily I say unto thee, to-day shalt thou be with Me in paradise." And now that there is an error somewhere, the question is, where is it? The truth is obvious, that is, that neither of the three saw or heard what transpired, but that Matthew and Mark were informed concerning the ill-treatment of the thieves without any discrimination between them, and that Luke was informed of both the ill-treatment of the one and the penitence of the other. And, notwithstanding that they may have faithfully recorded the matter as it came to them, it is evident that they cannot all be correct. Hence it is certain that the question embraced in the request of the thief and the answer of Jesus is not to be settled according to any particular phraseology, but according to the facts of the case. And therefore, considering the condition of the two, the fact that the Lord Jesus was about to give up the Ghost, and that the thief was expiating his crime beside Him, and fully realizing that he was soon to be numbered with the dead, it is evident that he looked forward to that glorious event which was the hope of Israel, the hope of Paul, the consolation of the afflicted Job, and the only thing that could satisfy David, and said, " Lord remember me when Thou comest into Thy kingdom." Thus there is nothing in or connected with the case to make it appear that the answer of Jesus was to the effect that upon that day he should be with Him in paradise. And the only thing that could have induced the present construction was the erroneous doctrine concerning the future state, and the only thing that has continued its existence in such a form has been the continuance of that same unreasonable and anti-scriptural idea that fills the fancies of so many thousands of the present day, to the almost utter exclusion of the fact that there will be such a thing as the reality of a resurrection. Thus it is evident that if the story as recorded by Luke be correct in fact, that the present construction is an error, and that the comma should be inserted after *day* instead of after *thee*, or, as would be more in accordance with the facts in the case, to render it thus: Because thou hast not followed the example of thy companion and hast spoken thus, I say unto thee, that thou shalt be with Me in paradise. But, be this as it may, there is none under the necessity of adhering to the present construction; so, as has been said, take out the comma, and all can judge for themselves, for this construction only constitutes or represents the idea of those who inserted it, and with this removed it will be easily seen that the request of the thief pointed to the resurrection from the dead, and that the answer of Jesus pointed with as much precision to the same great event. For the idea that death is an introduction to a future state is as precisely heathen as the resurrection of the dead is precisely Christian.

Those Who Have Fallen Asleep.

"Now, if Christ be preached that He rose from the dead, how say some among you that there is no resurrection of the dead? But if there be no resurrection of the dead, then is not Christ risen: And if Christ be not risen, then is our preaching vain, and your faith is also vain. Yea, and we are found false witnesses of God; because we have testified of God that He raised up Christ: whom He raised not up, if so be that the dead rise not. For if the dead rise not, then is not Christ raised: And if Christ be not raised, your faith is vain; ye are yet in your sins. Then they also which are fallen asleep in Christ are perished."—*I Corinthians, XV ch.*, 12*th to* 18*th vs.* If those who had fallen asleep in Christ had perished, if Christ had not risen, then the realities of salvation are embraced in and depend upon the resurrection, and are not consummated at death, or even begun. But that destruction or perishing which would be the inevitable result of no resurrection, is begun, yea, consummated; for if, in the absence of the resurrection, all the righteous even are to perish, the idea that men live after they are dead, and before they are resurrected, is altogether out of the question. For the language of the Apostle proves positively that in the absence of the resurrection they had perished. Now, if it were as so many teach, that at death the righteous go to heaven, notwithstanding that they place them in coffins and bury them in the grouud, as Paul very well knew they did; if they go to heaven and surround the throne of glory or become angels, how is it that Paul tells us such a story as this, that unless they were resurrected they had perished? Here he teaches plainly that those who had died were not angels or spirits, but that they were dead, and that unless they were resurrected they had perished. Aside from the resurrection, there was no future for them; their existence had ceased forever. For Christ, being the resurrection and life, without that resurrection and life those beings would never again exist. For the natural life having been spent and ceased, the bodies having returned to dust and the dust to the earth as it was, and the spirit to God, who gave it, the first requisite to a future existence was the resurrection or re-creation of those bodies, that they might receive the eternal spirit or be brought into existence by it, and thus again become living souls. Not natural bodies, the life of which is the blood, but spiritual bodies, the life of which is to be the eternal spirit, which is the eternal life. But those whose faith comes within the bounds of spiritualism and transmigration, based upon that heretical foundation which they call a glorious mystery, cannot accord with such plain teaching as this. For as men cannot serve God and mammon, neither can they believe truth and error, and thus it is nothing strange that they should lay aside or obscure the resurrection, for why should they want to be raised up at the last day? what do they want with that burdensome body or shell of corruption as they make it to appear? Why is it that they, having got out of it through the gate of death, and escaped to the realms of bliss, should think of returning to that earthly tenement from which they had such a glorious exit? No; the fact is, that their teachings are not in harmony with the resurrection, but are more in harmony with the teachings of the heathen general, who, when before the walls of Jerusalem, found it necessary to address his soldiers upon what he thought to be the immortality of the soul. And when one is honest enough to mark the similarity between the teachings of this Roman dignitary and the teachings of those who place the resurrection in obscurity, and teach that at death men become angels or spirits, that they pass to the celestial clime and receive their reward in heaven, it is hard for any one to believe their teachings in respect to the future state to be anything other than heathenism, as is plainly pictured in the following: When a breach had been made in the wall of the ill-fated Jerusalem, Titus, seeing that to carry his point by gaining possession of that breach, that loss of life, and perhaps to a great extent, was inevitable; that death stared in the face of those who dared to approach it, called around him his chosen warriors, and in substance thus addressed them: "Inasmuch as all men have to die, and inasmuch as those who are of a cowardly spirit are to be despised, and as it is only a question of a little time as to whether we die now or hereafter, and as to die gloriously ought to be the great object of our lives, it becomes you, notwithstanding that the achievement of this victory may cost the mortality of some of you, to display the valor and maintain the dignity of Roman soldiers, and thereby earn the reward of those who die gloriously. For *they become good demons and inherit the air called ether among the stars."* Thus Titus taught his soldiers that at death they would pass to the celestial clime, and there enjoy everlasting bliss, just as is taught, with few exceptions, from the pulpit of our day. And if Titus had directed the minds of his soldiers to the resurrection, then he would have been teaching them Scripture, but as it was he did not know or believe the Scriptures, and therefore he taught them that heathenism which, through the apostasy of the church, is so popularly taught at the present day, that is that at death the good pass from hence to the celestial regions and become angels, or, as Titus has it, *good spirits*, and receive their reward in the enjoyment of eternal felicity. This they teach with nothing but assertion and fancy to support it, while every sentence of Scripture that bears directly upon the subject is to the contrary. Now the question is, whose religion or what religion is this that is taught at the present day? Is it that which Titus taught, or that which Paul preached? For Christ says that he that believeth in Him He will raise him up at the last day. Titus says that they are up. And many of these modern believers will tell you in the most emphatic manner that their dead friends are angels in heaven. Thus the time seems to have come when men do not only love darkness rather than light, but when they have the audacity to come to the light with their darkness and tell us that it is light. But what a contrast between this darkness and this light which the Apostle casts upon the subject. For when Paul stood and answered for himself before King Agrippa, his efforts were to convince him and those who were with him, that the dead would rise, that there would be a resurrection of the dead; they were not to prove that the dead were alive in heaven, *for this was the difference between them*. The heathen believed in *spirits*, or the *spiritual existence* of those who had passed away, but Paul taught that they were dead, and that they would be *raised from the dead*. He taught them concerning his hope, and his hope was the hope of Israel, and the hope of Israel was the resurrection from the dead, and this was the hope of every primitive Christian, and they had no other hope; thus all that Scripture tells us of life hereafter is through the resurrection, and though blessed are the dead which die in the Lord, it is because they rest from their labors, for sleep is rest, and Christ called being dead asleep; thus this sleep that they sleep is their rest, for it is not the *living*, but the *dead*, that rest. And the reason why they are blessed is because they are that class of dead that die in the Lord. So that all that is death points to the grave, and all that is life points to the resurrection. And it seems that all ought to realize this fact when they look back and see the Lord Jesus as He stood before the people, declaring to the world that "He was the resurrection and the life, that the hour was coming in the which all that were in their graves should hear His voice and should come forth, they that had done good unto the resurrection of life, and they that had done evil unto the resurrection of damnation." And now, let heathen hope be what it may, this was the hope of Israel, this was the hope of Paul, the hope of every primitive Christian; there is no other hope. For if in the absence of the resurrection they that have fallen asleep in Christ have perished, it must require the resurrection to bring them to life that they perish not. But those who entertain the ideas of Titus do not care whether there be any resurrection or not, for as they suppose, or try to suppose, that at death they enter upon the realities of eternal life, it is all that they trouble themselves about. But what in language could more flatly contradict and more positively condemn such teachings, and prove them to be the offspring of heathenism in their origin, and contrary to anything that in truth might be called the reality of the Holy Scriptures, than the declaration of the Apostle that in the absence of the resurrection all who had fallen asleep in Christ had perished.

Dives and Lazarus.

"There was a certain rich man which was clothed in purple and fine linen, and fared sumptuously every day. And there was a certain beggar named Lazarus, which was laid at his gate, full of sores. And desired to be fed with the crumbs which fell from the rich man's table: Moreover the dogs came and licked his sores, And it came to pass, that the beggar died, and was carried by the angels into Abraham's bosom: the rich man also died and was buried; And in hell he lifted up his eyes, being in torments, and seeth Abraham afar off, and Lazarus in his bosom. And he cried, and said, Father Abraham, have mercy on me, and send Lazarus, that he may dip the tip of his finger in water, and cool my tongue; for I am tormented in this flame. But Abraham said, Son, remember that thou in thy lifetime receivedst thy good things, and likewise Lazarus evil things: but now he is comforted and thou art tormented. And beside all this, between us and you there is a great gulf fixed: so that they which would pass from hence to you cannot; neither can they pass to us, that would come from thence. Then he said, I pray thee therefore, father, that thou wouldst send him to my father's house: For I have five brethren; that he may testify unto them, lest they also come into this place of torment. Abraham saith unto him, They have Moses and the Prophets; let them hear them. And he said, Nay, Father Abraham: but if one went unto them from the dead, they will repent. And he said unto him, If they hear not Moses and the Prophets, neither will they be persuaded, though one rose from the dead."—*Luke XVI, from* 19*th v.*

The fact that this language is figurative is so plainly shown upon its face, and is so clearly taught by all the vital truths of Scripture, that to attempt to prove it such seems like striving to do that which is already done. But when we consider the fact that there are so many who accept its meaning as literal, and so few that regard it in the sense which it is intended, the first thing necessary to know is that it is figurative. It is figurative, first, because it represents the two extremes—wealth, with all that it could impart, and poverty in its lowest grade—as shown in the 19th and 20th verses. It is figurative, in that it shows how little the poor ask of the rich, and how ungratefully that little is often refused, as shown in the 21st verse. It is figurative in that it points to a time that is far in the future, as shown in the 22d and 23d verses; for the beggar was dead and the rich man was dead and buried, and the spirit does not go to hell, nor to Abraham, but to God who gave it. It is figurative in that it shows that with the termination of the natural life the destiny of man is fixed, and that there is not, there cannot be, any communication with the dead; and that for one that is dead to communicate with the living, he must first be raised from the dead—that is, be made to live again—as shown in the last five verses. And now, as regards the views of those who understand, or think they do, that there was a Dives and a Lazarus, and that they were the one in Abraham's bosom, and the other in hell; that they were in reality there, and that the conversation mentioned really took place, and that it is not figurative. In regard to these views it is only necessary to point to the fact that if it required the resurrection of Lazarus from the dead before he could testify to the brethren of Dives, it would require the resurrection of both Lazarus and Dives, to make their presence a reality in Abraham's bosom and in hell. And inasmuch as God has appointed a day in the which He will judge the world, what inconsistency to suppose that reward and punishment is to precede judgment. Hence, inasmuch as the distinction between the conditions of the two beings, each of which represented his class, is pictured so plainly, and periods of time and circumstances so remote are referred to, it is but common sense to accept its meaning as figurative. For Lazarus was about as literally in Abraham's bosom as Abraham saw Christ's day literally and was glad. And Dives was in hell about as much as Jonah was, or perhaps less, for Dives is represented as lifting up his eyes in hell and crying unto Abraham, and Jonah is represented as being in hell and crying to God, as he says: "Out of the belly of hell cried I, and thou heardest my voice." Therefore, this is one hell. And in Deuteronomy, XXIIId and 22d, we read of the lowest hell; and so there must be more than one. And in Isaiah, LVIIth and 9th, we read of one who had debased himself even unto hell. And this must surely be a different one from that of Jonah's. And, in Revelation, XXth and 13th, we read that the sea, and death, and hell delivered up the dead which were in them, and this most certainly is a different one from that which Jonah was in, for that was a hell that was a hell of the living, not of the dead. And, in the 20th verse, death and hell were cast into the lake of fire. And hence we may see the folly of supposing that a reality existed in the case of Dives and Lazarus. Yet there is a perdition for the workers of iniquity, a literal lake of fire, a reality of things that is to be after the last resurrection; and as that lake of fire is also called hell, it is evident that there is a figurative, as well as a literal signification of the term hell; for, as Christ tells us that God is able to destroy both *body and soul* in hell, and gives us plainly to understand that those who do not fear Him are *thus to be destroyed*, this, the lake of fire, is the hell in which they are to be destroyed. Hence, this being the hell in which they are to be destroyed, and being the only hell that denotes a reality of punishment, all others, if embracing the question of punishment, must be figurative in their signification.

Our Earthly House of this Tabernacle.

"For we know that if our earthly house of this tabernacle were dissolved, we have a building of God, a house not made with hands, eternal in the heavens. For in this we groan, earnestly desiring to be clothed upon with our house which is from heaven."—*II Corinthians, V ch.* "Our earthly house of this tabernacle" is no other than the world in which we live. For it is our tabernacle that has the house, which house is to be dissolved. But, notwithstanding its dissolution, we know that we have "a building of God, a house not made with hands, eternal in the heavens," and no matter what the opinions of men may be concerning that house, we know that we have it, and that when the present house of our tabernacle is dissolved, that it will be the next house of our tabernacle. "For in this we groan," that is, we ourselves groan, but in that we ourselves will not groan, therefore "we earnestly desire to be clothed upon with our house which is from heaven," that is, that eternal house which is now in heaven and is to come from heaven, "if so be that being clothed we shall not be found naked," or destitute of a house. "For we that are in this tabernacle do groan, being burdened," that is, this tabernacle which has the earthly house. "Not for that we would be unclothed," that is, not that our condition should be made worse, and that notwithstanding that in our natural lives we are burdened, we should desire that which is worse, even death, but we desire to be clothed upon "that mortality might be swallowed up of life." That is, that this earthly house of our tabernacle might be changed for the eternal one, which is now in heaven, with which Paul earnestly desired to be clothed upon, when it should come from heaven. And now, says Paul, "He that hath wrought us for the self-same thing is God, who also hath given us the earnest of the spirit." And the earnest of the spirit is a foretaste and witness of the life which is to be the result of our being clothed upon with our house which is from heaven, not that we were to go to heaven and get it, but it was to come from heaven to us. Then Paul says, "Therefore we are always confident, knowing that whilst we are at home in the body, we are absent from the Lord. (For we walk by faith, not by sight,) We are confident, I say, and willing rather to be absent from the body and to be present with the Lord." "At home in the body we are absent from the Lord." While we are in this natural state we are absent from the Lord, "but we walk by faith," and so look forward to that time when in an immortal state we shall be present with Him. "Wherefore we labor, that whether present or absent, we may be accepted of Him. For we must all appear before the judgment seat of Christ; that every one may receive the things done in the body, according to that he hath done, whether it be good or bad." "*Done in the body,*" that is, done in this life, which is represented by the term body, just as Paul meant when he said *at home in the body;* and how plainly this presents the fact that we cannot be mortal and immortal at the same time. For Paul desired not to be in the mortal but the immortal state, and shows us plainly that he had to be in the one or the other, by desiring that he might be clothed upon with his house from heaven, so that *mortality might be swallowed up of life.* That is, that he might change this natural or temporary life for the glorious realities of eternal life, and then he points us to the time when this is to be brought to pass. For, says he, "we must all appear before the judgment seat of Christ," which is to be preceded by the resurrection and personal presence of every soul, for we can be nowhere present except personal, for we are not spirits or spiritual beings, but personal beings, and as our presence here is the result of our being created, so our presence hereafter will be the result of our being resurrected or re-created.

Of Michael or the Michaels.

The unnatural idea of mystery concerning the nature of Christ, which is one of the plainest revelations of Scripture, has become so undaunted in its operations that, as a part of this mystery or mystical complication, Michael or the Michaels have been presented to the world as what might be properly termed the untransmigrated Christ. And therefore, it is proper that the nature and office of this or these caricatures should be seen and understood as they are prseented in the Sacred Volume; hence, in Daniel, Xth chapter, 12th and 13th verses, we read: " Then said he unto me, fear not, Daniel: for from the first day that thou didst set thine heart to understand, and to chasten thyself before thy God, thy words were heard, and I am come for thy words. But the prince of the kingdom of Persia withstood me one and twenty days: but lo, Michael, one of the chief princes, came to help me; and I remained there with the kings of Persia." Here we see that this Michael was one of the chief princes; that is, he was one of a number, all of whom were chief princes, and therefore he might have been one of ten, twenty, a hundred or a thousand, just such chief princes as he was. For this band to which he belonged was a band of chief princes, whose number is not defined. But the fact that he was one of a number just such as himself, is positively affirmed. Hence, if he had been the Messiah, there might have been a thousand more just such Messiahs as he. And " Michael, your prince," mentioned in the 21st verse, is that one of the chief princes mentioned in the 13th verse. And the reason why he was called his prince was because he was that one of the chief princes which was favoring and forwarding the business which particularly concerned Daniel. And when again it is said in chapter XIIth, 1st verse: " At that time shall Michael stand up, the great prince which standeth for the children of the people," it is the same Michael mentioned in the 13th and 21st verses of the Xth chapter, engaged in the same manner, attending to the same or similar business. So that this Michael of the XIIth chapter is the same one of the chief princes of which there might have been a thousand more just such as he. For had Michael been assigned some other position, and one of his fellows being appointed to his, they would call him Christ the same as they do Michael. And if any other one of the thousand had been appointed to occupy this particular position, he would be their Christ the same as the others. So that if any one of a thousand could be their Messiah, there could be a thousand as easily as one. Therefore we see how inglorious and foreign to anything that comes within the bounds of consistency is this so-called mystery concerning our Lord Jesus Christ. For they are not satisfied with teaching that there is one God, who is the Father of Jesus Christ, and that there is no God but the Father, that Jesus was the Son of Mary, and also the Eternal Son of God, and always was God, notwithstanding that there is no God but the Father, and that though God was the Father of Jesus, Jesus was the true Eternal God, and that notwithstanding that Jesus was the Son of the living and true God, He was that God whose Son He was; but they have added to this chaotic mass of heretical stupidity the idea that one of the chief princes also was Christ, to which number it is plain to be seen that they have opportunity to add a thousand more.

Melchisedec, the Order of Melchisedec, and Christ After His Order.

As saith the Apostle: "Though He were a Son, yet learned He obedience by the things which He suffered." So this Son learned obedience by suffering these things. (So, certainly He did not know it before, or else He would not have had it to learn.) And being made perfect (so He was not perfect before), He became the author of eternal salvation to all them that obey Him. "Called of God, a high priest after the order of Melchisedec." That is, after He had been made perfect by the things which He suffered, then it was that He became a high priest after the order of Melchisedec. Hence, no matter what the order of Melchisedec is, Christ is a priest after this order. Yet Christ had both father and mother, but Melchisedec had neither. Christ's descent, according to the flesh, was from David, but Melchisedec was without descent. Christ had beginning of days and end of life, but Melchisedec had neither. Thus it is plain that Christ was not such a being as Melchisedec, but a priest after the same order, who, after He had learned obedience by the things which he suffered, had died and had risen from the dead no more to die, death having no more dominion over Him, in eternity; He entered upon the office of high priest, and was as Melchisedec and after the same order. For Melchisedec had no affinity to time, he was a creature of eternity, he was a being whom God had created as angels are created, who have nothing to do with time. For time is but as a coil in eternity, which that same eternity absorbs as it is unrolled, until at last exhausted, eternity is the same eternity and time is no more. Thus time, being but a spot in eternity, whoever is created or exists independent of this world has nothing to do with days, but belongs to eternity. And this being after the order of Melchisedec is only as appertaining to His office as priest, which office He did not fill until He had been made perfect through His sufferings and after His resurrection. Hence, when He was done with time and entered upon eternity, He entered upon His office as high priest after the order of Melchisedec. For Melchisedec and this order being independent of time, Christ must of necessity enter upon eternity prior to His being a high priest after this order. Thus it is that Melchisedec was a being without father, mother or descent, without beginning of days or end of life. And thus Christ as a priest is a priest after this order.

The Apostles' Faith in Christ.

What the Apostles thought about the nature of Christ, or rather, what they knew, their faith in Him as inferred from what they said concerning Him, from what they told Jesus and what Jesus did not contradict but more fully explained, is shown in the conversation between Jesus and the two who journeyed from Jerusalem to Emmaus, when, in reply to His question concerning their conversation, Cleopas, answering, said unto Him, "Art Thou only a stranger in Jerusalem, and hast not known the things which are come to pass there in these days? And He said unto them, what things? And they said unto Him, concerning Jesus of Nazareth, which was a prophet mighty in deed and word before God and all the people: And how the chief priests and our rulers delivered Him to be condemned to death, and have crucified Him." This was their mournful story, and they manifested their despair by adding, "But we trusted that it had been He which should have redeemed Israel." Thus, when Jesus was among His disciples, they had a lively hope, for they supposed that He would restore the kingdom of Israel, and again establish the throne of David. They had followed Him through all the scenes that preceded the triumphant entry into

Jerusalem; they had witnessed His power, and saw the authority that He exercised in the Temple; they had looked upon Him as their Lord and Master, and through all their pilgrimage with Him they had never met with a failure. When they were needy their wants were supplied, when they were in difficulty it was always overcome. They had witnessed His miracles, they understood His power, they knew Him to be mighty in word and deed. He was the great one in whom all their hopes were concentrated. But after they had witnessed the scene in the garden they began to despair of that which they had hoped for, and, following Him to the judgment hall, and witnessing that which transpired there, their case became more hopeless still, and one even despaired and turned his back upon Him. But some, faithful to the last, followed Him to the crucifixion, and there beheld the last breathings of Him in whom all their hopes were concentrated, and then their hope was gone. Thus they realized their situation, because they understood the nature of death, that it was the end of life, and that between it and the resurrection there was no existence, and "they knew not the Scriptures that He was to rise again the third day." Now, if the ideas of the disciples concerning death had been in accordance with believers generally of the present day, their hope, instead of being gone, would have been strengthened, for they would have supposed that He had gone to heaven, that He had appeared in the presence of the Father, and was the mighty monarch reigning most gloriously, who soon would achieve for them all that their hopes embraced, and that they would soon be transported to that same glorious abode. But those who understood the nature of death and the realities of the teachings of their Lord and Master, did not look to heaven then for the object of their affections, but to the tomb of Joseph, where they knew they had lain Him. Moreover, there was no spiritualism connected with His case; there was no appearing, not the least shadow of Him; no manifestation, however faint, to denote an existence between His death and resurrection. No, there was not such a thing thought of; for when they sought Him they sought Him at the tomb, and when they missed Him it was their Lord that they missed. And the wonderful event of His resurrection, or His being brought to life again, transpired at the tomb. And to this being, whom they had laid in the tomb, was directed every thought that was expressed and every action connected with the case. There was not so much as a dream concerning His being alive between His death and resurrection. Thus we see that death absorbed all the hope of His disciples, that with His death it died. And hence the language of the Apostle, " He hath begotten us again unto a lively hope by the resurrection of Jesus Christ from the dead." And what nonsense it would be to talk of being begotten again unto a lively hope unless that hope was gone, for, if that hope had not been gone, it would not only not have been necessary but impossible to have begotten it again. But now, says the Apostle, "He hath begotten us again unto a lively hope by the resurrection of Jesus Christ from the dead;" thus showing that Jesus was dead and their hope gone, and that unless Jesus was resurrected they had no Saviour; that He had ceased to exist, and upon His resurrection depended His future existence, and that if He had not been resurrected He would have remained in the grave and this Holy One would have seen corruption. But David said, "Thou wilt not suffer Thine Holy One to see corruption." Thus it is that God hath begotten us again unto a lively hope, for He raised this Holy One from the dead so that He saw no corruption. Thus their hope that was lost in His death was renewed by His resurrection; thus we see that the loss of their hope was the result of death, and the renewing of their hope was the result of life; thus as life is a reality so death is a reality; the one is that which the other is not. And thus the disciples realized it, and thus they have taught that as life constitutes an existence, so death constitutes a non-existence.

The Death of Christ.

"And at the ninth hour Jesus cried with a loud voice, saying, 'Eloi, Eloi, Lama Sabachthani?' which is, being interpreted, My God, My God, why hast thou forsaken me?" And when He had cried again with a loud voice He gave up the ghost. Inasmuch as the nature of God, the nature of Christ and the nature of man have been subjects of special consideration, so this, the nature of death, as realized by our Saviour, should be especially understood. For it had not only the simple importance of death attached to it, but it embraced a significance peculiar only to itself, and was brought about through that peculiar operation by which His death became confirmatory of His teachings concerning the reality of His nature and life. For one of the great objects of His teachings was to convince His disciples and the world that He was not only man, but that He was also God, and that there were not two Gods, but that God was one, and that the God that He was was the Father in Him. As He taught when "Philip said unto Him, Lord, show us the Father, and it sufficeth us. Jesus saith unto him, Have I been so long time with you, and yet thou hast not known me, Philip? He that hath seen Me, hath seen the Father, and how sayest thou then, show us the Father? Believest thou not that I am in the Father, and the Father in Me? the words that I speak unto you, I speak not of Myself: but the Father that dwelleth in me, He doeth the works." Thus the great truth which Jesus endeavored to impress upon the minds of His followers was that He was in the Father, and that the Father was in Him; that they were the same one God. For it was not only that the Father was in the Son, but also that the Son was in the Father, thus showing the oneness of their existence. And again He endeavors to impress this truth upon their minds by exhorting them, when He says, " Believe Me that I am in the Father, and the Father in Me: or else believe Me for the very works' sake," which seems equivalent to saying that if you will not believe my words, believe the works that I do, for though man may speak the words that I speak, the works that I do it is impossible for man to do. Therefore, if according to my words ye will not believe that I am God, believe the works that I do which none but God can do, that ye may believe that I am in the Father, and that the Father is in Me; therefore when Christ hung upon the cross, and the natural life was nearly spent, He realized that which He had never realized before, and exclaimed: My God, My God, why hast thou forsaken Me? And when He had cried aloud again, immediately He gave up the ghost. Thus God forsook Him; His Divinity took its flight, and the being Jesus was dead. And this God that forsook Him was the Father which was in Him, and this being a part of Himself, He could no longer exist, but gave up the ghost, and was dead. And thus again God was God, and man was man, until the resurrection of that same Jesus Christ who through the eternal spirit had offered Himself a sacrifice, was raised by the power of that same Eternal God whose nature or self, then as before, constituted His Divinity; and thus *again*, though united to God and to man by being of the real nature of both, He was neither Mary nor Jehovah, but was Their Son Jesus Christ, His Own Self.

INDEX.

	Page.
Jesus Christ the Son of God, and the Son of Man	19
Jesus Christ what God, His Father, made Him	23
God, a Personal Being	25
God, the Father	32
The Spirit of God	35
The Oneness of the Two Distinct Beings	40
Free Agency and Foreordination	42
Jesus Christ's First Existence	45
In the Beginning was the Word	48
The World Knew Him Not	49
The Word was made Flesh	51
I Came Forth from the Father	53
For Thou Lovedst Me	56
Sent Into the World	58
Though He was Rich, yet for Our Sakes He became Poor.	62
The Falsity of being Equal to God	65
The Reality of that which is Taught in Collossians	66
Christ Glorified with His Father's Own Self	69
The Family of Jesus	72
The Mother of Jesus Christ	78
The Union of God and Man	80
Immortality	86
Faith	92
Predestination	95
Mystery	100
The Word	104
The Valley of Dry Bones	106
Resurrection	111

The Mind Not the Spirit	115
The Physiologist and the Mind	121
Conversion	128
Doubts After Conversion	138
Communion	140
Baptism	146
The Soul	159
The Spirit of Man	177
The Judgment and the Judge	183
The Devil, or Satan, and Hell	192
The Finale of the Earth, the Righteous and the Wicked..	196
How it was that Moses was at the Transfiguration	203
Who Preached to the Spirits in Prison	207
Of the Spirits in Prison	212
Christ's Answer to the Thief	216
Of Those who have Fallen Asleep	223
Dives and Lazarus	229
Our Earthly House of this Tabernacle	233
Of Michael or the Michaels	236
Melchisedec	239
What the Apostles Knew about the Nature of Christ	241
The Death of Christ	245

www.ingramcontent.com/pod-product-compliance
Lightning Source LLC
Chambersburg PA
CBHW020801230426
43666CB00007B/801